knitted wild animals

knitted wild animals

A collection of adorable animals to knit from scratch

Sarah Keen

GUILD OF MASTER CRAFTSMAN
PUBLICATIONS

First published 2009 by
Guild of Master Craftsman Publications Ltd
Castle Place, 166 High Street, Lewes,
East Sussex BN7 1XU

This edition published 2010

Text © Sarah Keen, 2009
Copyright in the Work © GMC Publications Ltd,
2009

Illustrations by Simon Rodway, except for those
on page 114 and at the right of page 122,
which are © Sarah Keen

ISBN 978-1-86108-670-9

A catalogue record for this book is available
from the British Library.

Associate Publisher: Jonathan Bailey
Production Manager: Jim Bulley
Managing Editor: Gerrie Purcell
Senior Project Editor: Dominique Page
Editor: Rachel Netherwood
Managing Art Editor: Gilda Pacitti
Design: Rebecca Mothersole

Set in Frutiger
Colour origination by GMC Reprographics
Printed and bound by Hung Hing Off-Set

I would like to thank the following people for their kindness and support:

Cynthia, Dr Ruth and Dr Nicholls;

Cheryl, Liz and Eirwen;

Maureen, Mary and Shirley.

Special thanks to my parents.

Special thanks also to Clare Wools, Aberystwyth, Wales,

and to Jonathan Bailey and all the team at GMC Publications.

Where those wild beasts hide

Introduction

I learned to knit as a child and have made numerous soft
toys, baby clothes and garments. I began experimenting with
calculating stitches and found it fascinating and so started writing
my own knitting patterns from scratch. I've experimented with
different arts and crafts but knitting, for me, is what I want to
do most of all.

This book started with the monkey and elephant and then grew
to be a book of 15 different wild animals. Hopefully there's
something in it that's appealing to all. I have enjoyed creating
these animals and hope you too will find enjoyment in whichever
pattern you decide to knit.

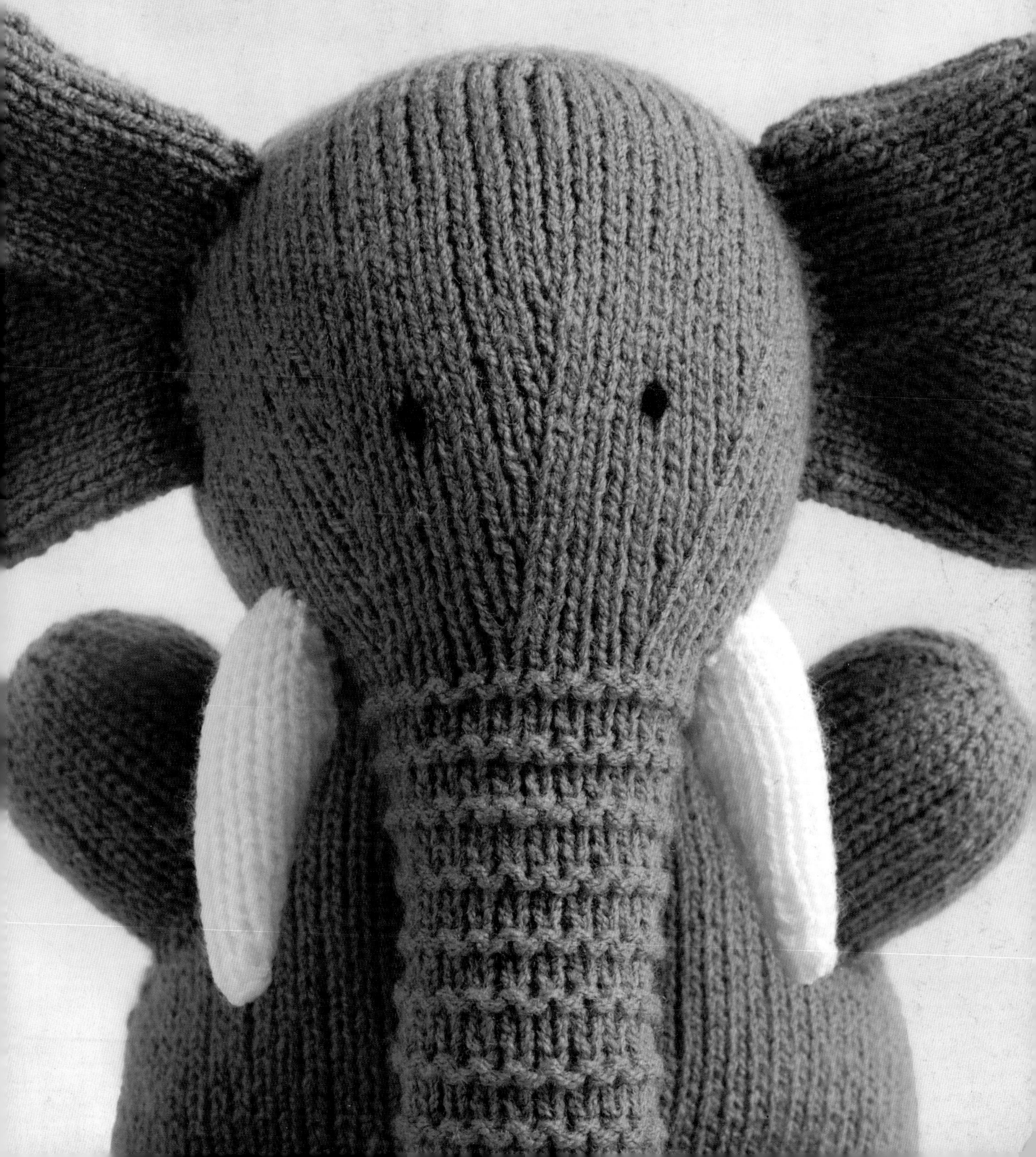

GIRAFFE >> 46

ZEBRA >> 52

66 << TIGER

RHINO >> 90

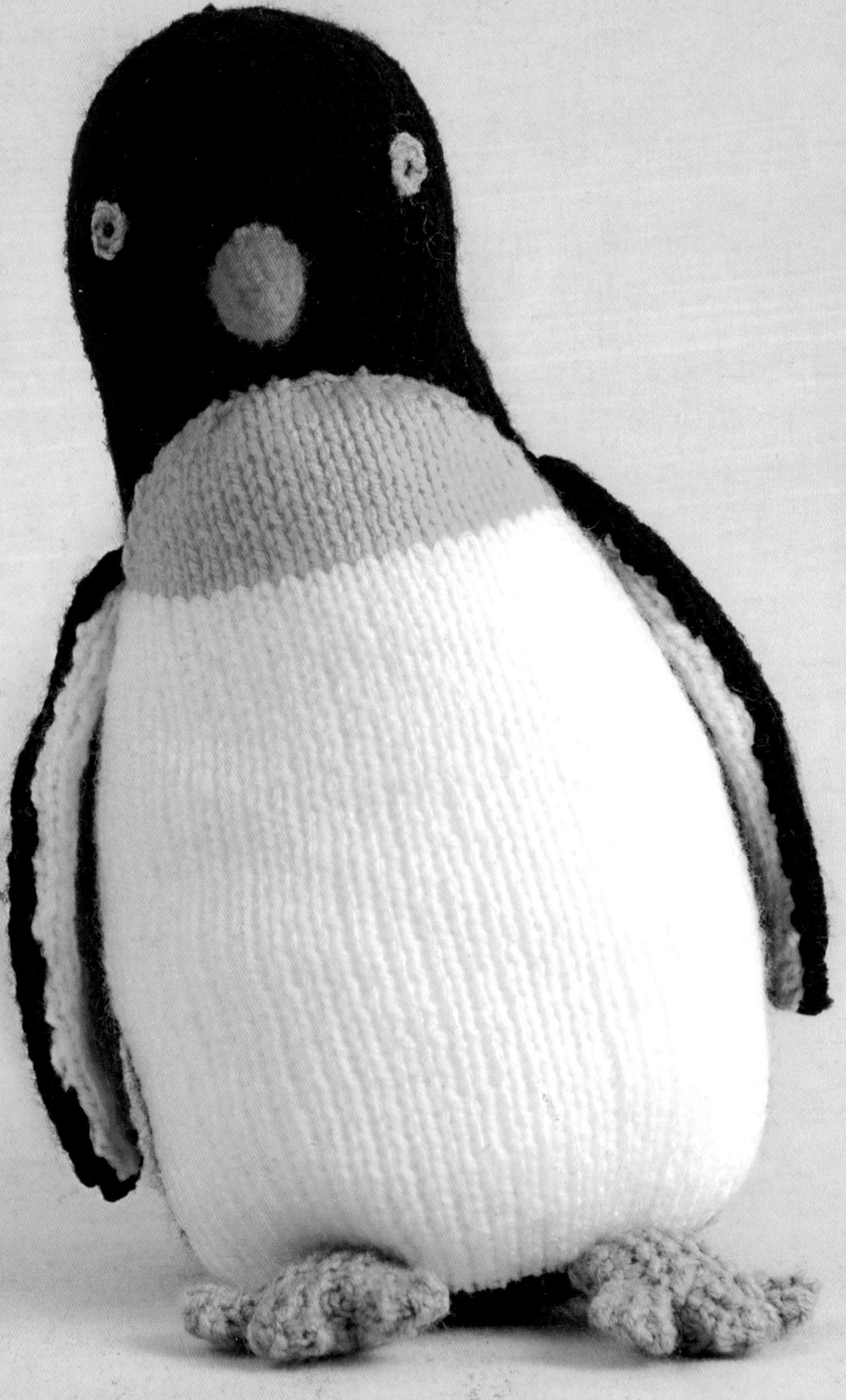

HIPPO >> 86

WARTHOG >> 94

A moose with many friends

Busy lions

Snakes you can trust

Absent-minded elephants

Just plain sensible monkeys

The beasts

Elephants take dust or mud baths to clean themselves and to protect their skin from the sun, wind and insects. Their skin is so sensitive that they can even feel a fly landing on it! Elephants love playing in water and drink around 30gals (113l) of it every day.

ELEPHANT

What you'll need

Measurement
Elephant measures 9½in (24cm) in height

Materials
Any DK yarn:
100g grey (A)
20g white (B)
Oddment of black for features
Note: amounts are generous
but approximate
A pair of 3.25mm (US3:UK10) needles
Acrylic toy stuffing
Plastic-headed marker pins
Tweezers for stuffing small parts (optional)

Tension
26 sts x 34 rows measure 4in (10cm) square
over stocking-st using 3.25mm needles
before stuffing

Abbreviations
See page 124

How to make Elephant

Body (make 2 pieces)
Beg at lower edge using the thumb method and A, cast on 35 sts.
First and next 4 foll alt rows: P.
Inc row: K10, m1, k15, m1, k10 (37 sts).
Inc row: K11, m1, k15, m1, k11 (39 sts).
Inc row: K12, m1, k15, m1, k12 (41 sts).
Inc row: K13, m1, k15, m1, k13 (43 sts).
Inc row: K14, m1, k15, m1, k14 (45 sts).
Beg with a p row, stocking-st 11 rows.
Dec row: K2tog, k to last 2 sts, k2tog tbl.
Next row: P.
Rep last 2 rows 12 more times (19 sts).
Cast off.

Base
Using the thumb method and A, cast on 20 sts.
First row: P.
Inc row: K1, m1, k to last st, m1, k1.
Rep first 2 rows 5 more times (32 sts).
Beg with a p row, stocking-st 5 rows.
Dec row: K2tog, k to last 2 sts, k2tog tbl.
Next row: P.
Rep last 2 rows 5 more times (20 sts).
Cast off.

Hind legs (make 2)
Using the thumb method and A, cast on 32 sts.
Beg with a p row, stocking-st 21 rows.
Dec row: (K2, k2tog) to end (24 sts).
Next and next foll alt row: P
Dec row: (K1, k2tog) to end (16 sts).
Dec row: (K2tog) to end (8 sts).
Thread yarn through rem sts, pull tight and secure.

Forelegs (make 2)
Using the thumb method and A, cast on 28 sts.
Beg with a p row, stocking-st 15 rows.
Dec row: (k2tog) 3 times, k2, (k2tog) 6 times, k2, (k2tog) 3 times (16 sts).
P 1 row.
Cast off.

Head
Beg at back using the thumb method and A, cast on 12 sts.
First and next 8 foll alt rows: P.
Inc row: (Inc) to end (24 sts).
Inc row: (K3, inc) to end (30 sts).
Inc row: (K4, inc) to end (36 sts).
Inc row: (K5, inc) to end (42 sts).
Inc row: (K6, inc) to end (48 sts).
Inc row: (K7, inc) to end (54 sts).
Inc row: (K8, inc) to end (60 sts).
Inc row: (K9, inc) to end (66 sts).
Inc row: (K10, inc) to end (72 sts).
Beg with a p row, stocking-st 15 rows.
Dec row: (K7, k2tog) to end (64 sts).
Next row: P50, turn.
Next row: S1k, k35, turn.
Next row: S1p, p to end.
Dec row: (K6, k2tog) to end (56 sts).
Next row: P44, turn.
Next row: S1k, k31, turn.
Next row: S1p, p to end.
Dec row: (K5, k2tog) to end (48 sts).
Next row: P38, turn.
Next row: S1k, k27, turn.
Next row: S1p, p to end.
Dec row: (K4, k2tog) to end (40 sts).
Next row: P32, turn.
Next row: S1k, k23, turn.
Next row: S1p, p to end.
Dec row: (K3, k2tog) to end (32 sts).
Next row: P.

Next 2 rows: K.
Dec row: K2tog, k to last 2 sts, k2tog tbl.
Rep last 4 rows 4 more times (22 sts).
Next row: P.
Next 3 rows: K.
Rep last 4 rows 8 more times.
P 1 row.
Dec row: K2, (k2tog) 4 times, k2, (k2tog) 4 times, k2 (14 sts).
Cast off p-wise.

Ears
Side 1 (make 2 pieces)
Using the thumb method and A, cast on 16 sts.
First and next 10 foll alt rows: P.
Inc row: K1, m1, k8, m1, k6, m1, k1 (19 sts).
Inc row: K10, m1, k9 (20 sts).
Inc row: K10, m1, k10 (21 sts).
Inc row: K10, m1, k11 (22 sts.
Inc row: K10, m1, k12 (23 sts).
Inc row: K10, m1, k13 (24 sts).
Inc row: K10, m1, k14 (25 sts).
Inc row: K10, m1, k15 (26 sts).
Shape next row: K2tog, k8, m1, k14, k2tog tbl (25 sts).
Shape next row: K2tog, k7, m1, k14, k2tog tbl (24 sts).
Shape next row: K2tog, k6, m1, k14, k2tog tbl (23 sts).
Dec row: P2tog tbl, p to last 2 sts, p2tog (21 sts).
Cast off.
Side 2 (make 2 pieces)
Using the thumb method and A, cast on 16 sts.
First and next 10 foll alt rows: P.
Inc row: K1, m1, k6, m1, k8, m1 k1 (19 sts).

Inc row: K9, m1, k10 (20 sts).
Inc row: K10, m1, k10 (21 sts).
Inc row: K11, m1, k10 (22 sts).
Inc row: K12, m1, k10 (23 sts).
Inc row: K13, m1, k10 (24 sts).
Inc row: K14, m1, k10 (25 sts).
Inc row: K15, m1, k10 (26 sts).
Shape next row: K2tog, k14, m1, k8, k2tog tbl (25 sts).
Shape next row: K2tog, k14, m1, k7, k2tog tbl (24 sts).
Shape next row: K2tog, k14, m1, k6, k2tog tbl (23 sts).
Dec row: P2tog tbl, p to last 2 sts, p2tog (21 sts).
Cast off.

Tusks (make 2)
Using the thumb method and B, cast on 4 sts.
Inc row: P this row increasing p-wise into first and last st.
Inc row: K this row increasing k-wise into first and last st.
Rep last 2 rows once (12 sts).
Beg with a p row, stocking-st 16 rows decreasing one st at each end of 4th and every foll 4th row (4 sts).
P 1 row.
Thread yarn through sts, pull tight and secure.

Making up
Body
Place two halves of body together matching all edges and join row-ends. Stuff body leaving neck and lower edge open.

Base
Pin base to lower edge of body and sew base to body all the way round, adding more stuffing to base if needed.

Hind legs
Join row-ends of hind legs and stuff. Stand body on flat surface and position legs wide apart, pin and sew cast-on sts of legs to body all the way round.

Forelegs
Fold cast-off sts in half and over-sew. Join row-ends and stuff. Pin each foreleg to either side of body pinning top of arm to 6th row below cast-off sts at neck. Sew cast-on sts in place all the way round.

Head
Gather round cast-on sts of head, pull tight and secure. Join row-ends of trunk and with seam at centre back, over-sew cast-off sts. Stuff trunk and join row-ends of head leaving a gap. Stuff head and close gap. Pin head to body, pinning first garter-st row of trunk to neck at centre front, adding more stuffing to neck if needed. Sew head to body by taking a small horizontal st from head and then a small horizontal st from body and do this alternately all the way round.

Ears
With right sides facing, place a side 1 and side 2 together matching all edges. Join row-ends and cast-off sts by sewing back and forth 1 st in from edge. Turn right-side out and catch cast-on sts together. Repeat for the other ear. Sew ears to head.

Tusks
Join row-ends of tusks from tips to beg of increase sts, and stuff, pushing stuffing in with tweezers or tip of scissors. Sew tusks to either side of head at top of trunk.

Embroidering the features
To make eyes, tie a knot in 2 lengths of black yarn, winding the yarn round 6 times to make each knot (see page 122). Check that the knots are the same size. Tie eyes to 15th row above top of trunk with 8 clear knitted sts in between. Run ends into head.

Tail
Take 6 lengths of yarn, each 16in (40cm) long, in a bundle and tie a knot in the centre. Fold in half and divide into 3. Plait for 1¼in (3cm) and tie a knot to secure. Cut ends ⅝in (1.5cm) from the knot. Sew tail to elephant at back.

The giraffe is the world's tallest animal and can grow up to 18ft (5.5m) high with feet the size of dinner plates. They sleep standing up for just 10 minutes to two hours each day! Newborn giraffe calves begin their lives by falling 6ft (2m) to the ground, head first... Bump!!!

GIRAFFE

DID YOU KNOW?
The mighty giraffe can drink 12gals (45.5l) in one sitting... Thirsty giraffe!

What you'll need

Measurement
Giraffe measures 10in (26cm) in height

Materials
Any DK yarn:
50g brown (A)
50g yellow (B)
25g cream (C)
Oddment of black for features
Note: amounts are generous
but approximate
A pair of 3.25mm (US3:UK10) needles
Acrylic toy stuffing
Plastic-headed marker pins

Tension
26 sts x 34 rows measure 4in (10cm) square
over stocking-st using 3.25mm needles
before stuffing

Pattern notes
Before beginning to knit, wind yarns A and
B into two separate balls

Abbreviations
See page 124

giraffe

Our giraffe asks whether sleeping standing up is really such a good idea?

Giraffes are fastidious about their hair;
they never leave the house without at
least one Afro comb.

How to make Giraffe
Body (make 2 pieces)

Note: two separate balls of A and B
are required

Beg at the lower edge. Using the thumb
method and one strand of A, cast on
35 sts.

First and next foll 4 alt rows: P.
Inc row: K10, m1, k15, m1, k10 (37 sts).
Inc row: K11, m1, k15, m1, k11 (39 sts).
Inc row: K12, m1, k15, m1, k12 (41 sts).
Inc row: K13, m1, k15, m1, k13 (43 sts).
Inc row: K14, m1, k15, m1, k14 (45 sts).
Next row: P.

Join in B and second ball of A and work
in blocks of colour, using a separate
ball for each block and twisting when
changing yarn.

Pattern
Row 1: K, using B.
Row 2: P2-A (second ball), p41-B, p2-A
(first ball).
Row 3: K4-A, k37-B, k4-A.
Row 4: P5-A, p35-B, p5-A.
Row 5: K2tog, k5-A, k31-B, k5, k2tog tbl-A
(43 sts).
Row 6: P7-A, p29-B, p7-A.

Row 7: K2tog, k7-A, k25-B, k7, k2tog tbl-A
(41 sts).
Row 8: P9-A, p23-B, p9-A.
Row 9: K2tog, k9-A, k19-B, k9, k2tog tbl-A
(39 sts).
Row 10: P11-A, p17-B, p11-A.
Row 11: K2tog, k11-A, k13-B, k11, k2tog
tbl-A (37 sts).
Row 12: P13-A, p11-B, p13-A.
Row 13: K2tog, k13-A, k7-B, k13, k2tog
tbl-A (35 sts).
Row 14: P15-A, p5-B, p15-A.
Row 15: K2tog, k15-A, k1-B, k15, k2tog
tbl-A (33 sts).

Row 16: P-A (second ball).
Row 17: K2tog, k13-A, k3-B, k13, k2tog tbl-A (31 sts).
Row 18: P13-A, p5-B, p13-A.
Row 19: K2tog, k10-A, k7-B, k10, k2tog tbl-A (29 sts).
Row 20: P10-A, p9-B, p10-A.
Row 21: K2tog, k7-A, k11-B, k7, k2tog tbl-A (27 sts).
Row 22: P7-A, p13-B, p7-A.
Row 23: K2tog, k4-A, k15-B, k4, k2tog tbl-A (25 sts).
Row 24: P4-A, p17-B, p4-A.
Row 25: K2tog, k1-A, k19-B, k1, k2tog tbl-A (23 sts).
Break off A and cont in B.
Rows 26, 28, 30 and 32: P.
Rows 27, 29, 31 and 33: K2tog, k to last 2 sts, k2tog tbl.
15 sts now rem with WS facing for next row.
Change to A.
Row 34: P-A.
Row 35: K2tog, k to last 2 sts, k2tog tbl-A (13 sts).
Rows 36 and 38: P-A.
Rows 37 and 39: K-A.
Join in 2 balls of B.
Row 40: P2-B, p9-A, p2-B (second ball).
Row 41: K3-B, k7-A, k3-B.
Row 42: P4-B, p5-A, p4-B.
Row 43: K5-B, k3-A, k5-B.
Row 44: P6-B, p1-A, p6-B.
Row 45: K-B (first ball).
Row 46: P6-B, p1-A, p6-B.
Row 47: K5-B, k3-A, k5-B.
Row 48: P4-B, p5-A, p4-B.
Row 49: K3-B, k7-A, k3-B.
Row 50: P2-B, p9-A, p2-B.
Cont in A, stocking-st 6 rows.
Cast off.

Base
Using the thumb method and A, cast on 20 sts.
First row: P.
Inc row: K1, m1, k to last st, m1, k1.
Rep these 2 rows 5 times more (32 sts).
Beg with a p row, stocking-st 5 rows.
Dec row: K2tog, k to last 2 sts, k2tog tbl.
Next row: P.
Rep last 2 rows 5 times more (20 sts).
Cast off.

Hind legs (make 2)
Beg at hoof using the thumb method and C, cast on 6 sts.
P 1 row.
Inc row: (Inc) to end.
Rep last 2 rows once (24 sts).
P 1 row.
Work 2 rows in garter-st.
Beg with a k row, stocking-st 2 rows.
Dec row: (K1, k2tog) to end (16 sts).
Beg with a p row, stocking-st 5 rows.
Change to A.
Dec row: (K2tog) to end (8 sts).
P 1 row.
Inc row: K1, (m1, k1) to end (15 sts).
P 1 row.
Inc row: (K1, m1, k1, m1, k1) to end (25 sts).
Beg with a p row, stocking-st 11 rows.
Change to B and stocking-st 10 rows.
Dec row: K1, (k2tog, k1) to end (17 sts).
P 1 row.
Cast off.

Forelegs (make 2)
Beg at hoof using the thumb method and C, cast on 6 sts.
P 1 row.
Inc row: (Inc) to end.
Rep last 2 rows once (24 sts).
P 1 row.
Garter-st 2 rows.

Beg with a k row, stocking-st 2 rows.
Dec row: (K1, k2tog) to end (16 sts).
Beg with a p row, stocking-st 5 rows.
Change to B.
Dec row: (K2tog) to end (8 sts).
P 1 row.
Inc row: K1, (m1, k1) to end (15 sts).
P 1 row.
Inc row: K3, (m1, k3) to end (19 sts).
Beg with a p row, stocking-st 11 rows.
Change to A and stocking-st 10 rows.
Dec row: K3, (k2tog) twice, k5, (k2tog) twice, k3 (15 sts).
P 1 row.
Dec row: K2, (k2tog) twice, k3, (k2tog) twice, k2 (11 sts).
P 1 row.
Cast off.

Head
Note: 2 separate balls of B are required.
Beg at centre back using the thumb method and A, cast on 8 sts.
First and next foll 3 alt rows: P.
Inc row: (Inc) to end (16 sts).
Inc row: (K1, inc) to end (24 sts).
Inc row: (K2, inc) to end (32 sts).
Inc row: (K3, inc) to end (40 sts).
Beg with a p row, stocking-st 7 rows.
Break yarn. Join on A and 2 balls of B as required and work in blocks of colour, using a separate ball for each block and twisting when changing yarn.
Shape head
Row 1: K2tog, k7-B, k22-A, k7, k2tog tbl-B (second ball) (38 sts).
Row 2: P10-B, p18-A, p10-B.
Row 3: K2tog, k10-B, k14-A, k10, k2tog tbl-B (36 sts).
Row 4: P13-B, p10-A, p13-B.
Row 5: K2tog, k13-B, k6-A, k13, k2tog tbl-B (34 sts).
Row 6: P16-B, p2-A, p16-B.

Row 7: K2tog, k to last 2 sts, k2tog tbl-B (first ball) (32 sts).
Row 8: P15-B, p2-A, p15-B.
Row 9: K2tog, k12-B, k4-A, k12, k2tog tbl-B (30 sts).
Row 10: P13-B, p4-A, p13-B.
Row 11: K2tog, k10-B, k6-A, k10, k2tog tbl-B (28 sts).
Row 12: P2tog tbl, p9-B, p6-A, p9, p2tog-B (26 sts).
Row 13: K2tog, k7-B, k8-A, k7, k2tog tbl-B (24 sts).
Row 14: P2tog tbl, p6-B, p8-A, p6, p2tog-B (22 sts).
Row 15: K2tog, k4-B, k10-A, k4, k2tog tbl-B (20 sts).
Row 16: P5-B, p10-A, p5-B.
Change to C.
Dec row: K3, (k2tog) twice, k6, (k2tog) twice, k3 (16 sts).
Beg with a p row, stocking-st 5 rows.
Dec row: K1, (k2tog, k1) to end (11 sts).
P 1 row.
Cast off.

Ears (make 2)

Using the thumb method and A, cast on 8 sts.
P 1 row.
Inc row: K1, (m1, k1) to end (15 sts).
Beg with a p row, stocking-st 3 rows.
Dec row: (K1, k2tog) to end (10 sts).
Beg with a p row, stocking-st 5 rows.
Dec row: (K2tog) to end (5 sts).
Thread yarn through rem sts, pull tight and secure.

Inside ear piece (make 2)

Using the thumb method and B, cast on 6 sts.
P 1 row.
Inc row: K2, (m1, k2) twice (8 sts).
Beg with a p row, stocking-st 3 rows.
Dec row: K2tog, k to last 2 sts, k2tog tbl.
Next row: P.
Rep last 2 rows once (4 sts).
Thread yarn through rem sts, pull tight and secure.

Horns (make 2)

Using the thumb method and A, cast on 8 sts.
Beg with a p row, stocking-st 4 rows ending on a k row.
Change to C and p 1 row.
Inc row: K1, (m1, k1) to end (15 sts).
Beg with a p row, stocking-st 3 rows.
Dec row: (K1, k2tog) to end (10 sts).
Thread yarn through rem sts and leave loose.

Mane

Special abbreviation: loop-st
Insert RH needle into next st, place first finger of LH behind LH needle and wind yarn round needle and finger twice, then just round needle once. Knit st, pulling 3 loops through. Place these loops on LH needle and knit into the back of them. Pull loops sharply down to secure. Cont to next s
Using B, cast on 10 sts loosely.
First row: K1, (loop-st) to last st, k1.
K 1 row.
Rep first row once.
Cast off.

Tail

Note: two separate balls of B are required.
Using the thumb method and A, cast on 15 sts.
Join in 2 balls of B and work in blocks of colour, using a separate ball for each block and twisting when changing yarn.
Row 1: P2-B, p11-A, p2-B.
Row 2: K3-B, k9-A, k3-B.
Row 3: P4-B, p7-A, p4-B.
Row 4: K5-B, k5-A, k5-B.
Row 5: P6-B, p3-A, p6-B.
Row 6: K7-B, k1-A, k7-B.
Row 7: P across all sts-B (second ball).
Row 8: K7-B, k1-A, k7-B.
Row 9: P6-B, p3-A, p6-B.
Row 10: K5-B, k5-A, k5-B.
Row 11: P4-B, p7-A, p4-B.
Row 12: K3-B, k9-A, k3-B.
Row 13: P2-B, p11-A, p2-B.
Row 14: K 1 row-A.
Change to C and p 9 rows.
Dec row: (K1, k2tog) to end (10 sts).
Thread yarn through rem sts, pull tight and secure.

Making up

Body
Place the two halves of body together matching all edges and join row-ends. Stuff body, leaving neck and lower edge open.

Base
Pin base to lower edge of body and sew all the way round, adding more stuffing if needed.

Hind legs
Gather round cast-on sts of hooves, pull tight and secure. Stuff and join row-ends of hooves. Join row-ends of legs on right side using mattress stitch. Stuff legs. Place body on a flat surface, pin legs to body and sew cast-off sts of legs to body all the way round.

Forelegs
Work as for hind legs leaving gap to stuff. Stuff, close gap and with seam at centre inside edge, over-sew cast-off sts. Sew cast-off sts of forelegs to base of neck at each side.

Head
Join row ends of muzzle and with seam at centre of underneath, join cast-off sts. Gather round cast-on sts, pull tight and secure. Join row-ends leaving a gap, stuff and close gap. Pin head to body, adding more stuffing to neck if needed. Attach head to body by taking a small horizontal st from head, then a small horizontal st from body. Do this alternately all the way round.

Ears
With wrong sides together, place inside ear piece down the centre of ears, matching cast-on sts and allowing edges of ears to roll towards the centre. Sew in place and attach ears to head at each side.

DID YOU KNOW?
The name 'giraffe' comes from the Arabic word 'zarafah' meaning 'one who walks swiftly'.

Horns
Roll each horn up from one set of row-ends to the other. Pull sts on thread tight and slip-stitch in place. Attach horns to head between ears.

Embroidering the features
To make eyes, tie a knot in 2 lengths of black yarn winding yarn round 6 times to make each knot (see page 122). Check that the knots are the same size. Tie eyes to head halfway down, with 5 clear sts between. Run ends into head. Embroider nostrils in black taking 2 long sts. To begin and fasten off invisibly for the embroidery, tie a knot in the end of yarn and take a large st through work coming up to begin embroidery. Allow knot to disappear through knitting and be caught in stuffing. To fasten off, sew a few sts back and forth through work, inserting the needle where the yarn comes out.

Mane
Join cast-on and cast-off sts of mane. Place across head behind ears and sew all edges of mane to head.

Tail
Join row-ends of tail and stuff. Sew cast-on sts to body at centre back all the way round.

Each zebra has its unique stripe pattern – like human fingerprints. Some even have brown stripes. They also greet friends with a unique 'smile'. Zebras are members of the horse family. They have excellent hearing and eyesight and can run at speeds of up to 35mph (56kph).

ZEBRA

What you'll need

Measurement
Zebra measures 9½in (24cm) in height

Materials
Any DK yarn:
50g black (A)
50g white (B)
Note: amounts are generous but approximate
A pair of 3.25mm (US3:UK10) needles
Acrylic toy stuffing
Plastic-headed marker pins

Tension
26 sts x 34 rows measure 4in (10cm) square over stocking-st using 3.25mm needles before stuffing

Abbreviations
See page 124

Our zebra's tail is tufted at the end.
This makes him pretty special.

How to make Zebra

Body (make 2 pieces)
Beg at lower edge using the thumb method and A, cast on 35 sts.

First and next foll alt row: P.

Inc row: K10, m1, k15, m1, k10 (37 sts).

Join on B and work in stripe carrying yarn loosely up side of work, working the next 4 rows in B and then work 4 rows in A, doing this alternately throughout whilst shaping as follows:

Inc row: K11, m1, k15, m1, k11 (39 sts).

Next and next 2 foll alt rows: P.

Inc row: K12, m1, k15, m1, k12 (41 sts).

Inc row: K13, m1, k15, m1, k13 (43 sts).

Inc row: K14, m1, k15, m1, k14 (45 sts).

Beg with a p row, stocking-st 9 rows.

Dec row: K2tog, k to last 2 sts, k2tog tbl.

Next row: P.

Rep last 2 rows 14 more times (15 sts).

Stocking-st 2 rows straight.

Cast off in A.

Base
Using the thumb method and A, cast on 20 sts.

First row: P.

Inc row: K1, m1, k to last st, m1, k1.

Rep first 2 rows 5 more times (32 sts).

Beg with a p row stocking-st 5 rows.

Dec row: K2tog, k to last 2 sts, k2tog tbl.

Next row: P.

Rep last 2 rows 5 more times (20 sts).

Cast off.

Hind legs (make 2)
Beg at hoof using the thumb method and A, cast on 6 sts.

First row: P.

Inc row: (Inc) to end.

Rep first 2 rows once (24 sts).

Next and next foll alt row: P.

Inc row: (K1, inc) to end (36 sts).

Garter-st 2 rows.

Beg with a k row, stocking-st 2 rows.

Dec row: (K2, k2tog) to end (27 sts).

Beg with a p row stocking-st 3 rows.

Dec row: (K1, k2tog) to end (18 sts).

Beg with a p row stocking-st 3 rows.

Join on B and work in stripe carrying yarn loosely up side of work, working the next 4 rows in B and then work 4 rows in A, doing this alternately throughout whilst shaping as follows:

Dec row: (K2tog) to end (9 sts).

P 1 row.

Inc row: K1, (m1, k1) to end (17 sts).

Beg with a p row, stocking-st 3 rows.

Inc row: K1, (m1, k1) to end (33 sts).

P 1 row.

Work 22 rows in stripe, beg with 4 rows B and finishing with 2 rows A.

Cont in A.

Dec row: (K1, k2tog) to end (22 sts).

P 1 row.

Cast off.

Forelegs (make 2)
Beg at hoof using the thumb method and A, cast on 6 sts.

First row: P.

Inc row: (Inc) to end.

Rep first 2 rows once (24 sts).

P 1 row.

Garter-st 2 rows.

Beg with a k row, stocking-st 2 rows.

Dec row: (K1, k2tog) to end (16 sts).

Join on B and work in stripe carrying yarn loosely up side of work, working the next 4 rows in B and then work 4 rows in A, doing this alternately throughout whilst shaping as follows:

Dec row: (K2tog) to end (8 sts).

P 1 row.

Inc row: K1, (m1, k1) to end (15 sts).

Beg with a p row, stocking-st 3 rows.

Inc row: K3, (m1, k3) to end (19 sts).

P 1 row.

Work 28 rows in stripe beg with 4 rows B and finishing with 4 rows B.

Continue in A.

Dec row: K3, (k2tog) twice, k5, (k2tog) twice, k3 (15 sts).

P 1 row.

Dec row: K2, (k2tog) twice, k3, (k2tog) twice, k2 (11 sts).

P 1 row.

Cast off in A.

Head
Beg at back of head using the thumb method and A, cast on 9 sts.

First and next 4 foll alt rows: P.

Inc row: (Inc) to end (18 sts).

Inc row: (K1, inc) to end (27 sts).

Inc row: (K2, inc) to end (36 sts).

Inc row: (K3, inc) to end (45 sts).

Inc row: (K4, inc) to end (54 sts).

Beg with a p row, stocking-st 5 rows.

Join on B and work in stripe carrying yarn loosely up side of work, working the next 4 rows in B and then work 4 rows in A, doing this alternately throughout.

Work 12 rows in stripe.

Continue in stripe and decrease

Dec row: (K4, k2tog) to end (45 sts).

Beg with a p row, stocking-st 3 rows.

Dec row: (K3, k2tog) to end (36 sts).

Beg with a p row, stocking-st 3 rows.

Dec row: (K2, k2tog) to end (27 sts).

Beg with a p row, stocking-st 3 rows.

Cont in B.

Stocking-st 6 rows.

Dec row: K3, (k2tog) 4 times, k5, (k2tog) 4 times, k3 (19 sts).

P 1 row.

Cast off.

Ears (make 2)
Beg at lower edge using the thumb method and B, cast on 10 sts.
P 1 row.
Inc row: K2, (m1, k2) to end (14 sts).
Beg with a p row, stocking-st 2 rows, ending on a k row.
Change to A.
P 1 row.
Dec row: K2, (k2tog, k2) to end (11 sts).
Beg with a p row, stocking-st 3 rows.
Dec row: (K2tog) twice, k3, (k2tog) twice (7 sts).
Dec row: P1, (p2tog, p1) twice (5 sts).
Thread yarn through rem sts, pull tight and secure.

Mane
Special abbreviation: loop-st
Insert RH needle into next st, place first finger of LH behind LH needle and wind yarn round needle and finger twice, then just round needle once. Knit st, pulling 3 loops through. Place these loops on LH needle and knit into the back of them. Pull loops sharply down to secure. Cont to next st.
Using A, cast on 12 sts loosely.
First row: K1, (loop-st) to last st, k1.
K 1 row.
Rep first row once.
Cast off.

Tail
Beg at base using the thumb method and B, cast on 8 sts.
Beg with a p row, stocking-st 3 rows.
Join on A and work in stripe carrying yarn loosely up side of work.
Stocking-st 4 rows A.
Stocking-st 4 rows B.

Cont in A.
Garter-st 7 rows.
Cast off k-wise.

Making up
Body
Place the two halves of body together matching all edges and join row-ends. Stuff body leaving neck and lower edge open.

Base
Pin base to lower edge of body and sew base to body all the way round, adding more stuffing to base if needed.

Hind legs
Gather round cast-on sts of hooves, pull tight and secure. Stuff and join row-ends of each hoof. Join row-ends of legs on right side using mattress-stitch. Stuff legs. Place body on a flat surface, pin legs to body and sew cast-off sts of legs to body all the way round.

Forelegs
Work as for hind legs leaving gap to add stuffing. With seam at centre of inside, over-sew cast-off sts. Stuff and close gap and sew cast-off sts of forelegs to second black stripe down from neck at each side.

Head
Gather round cast-on sts of head, pull tight then secure. Join row-ends leaving a gap and with seam at centre of underneath, over-sew cast-off sts. Stuff and close gap. Pin head to body adding more stuffing to neck if needed. Stitch head to body by taking a small horizontal st from head, then a small horizontal st from body and do this alternately all the way round.

Ears
Join row-ends of ears and with seams at centre back, sew ears to white stripe on head with ears pointing outwards.

Embroidering the features
To make eyes, tie a knot in 2 lengths of black yarn winding the yarn round 6 times to make each knot (see page 122). Check that the knots are the same size. Tie eyes to white stripe of head with 7 clear knitted sts in between. Run ends into head. Embroider nostrils in black taking 2 long sts. To begin and fasten off invisibly for the embroidery, tie a knot in the end of yarn and take a large st through work coming up to begin embroidery. Allow knot to disappear through knitting and be caught in stuffing. To fasten off, sew a few sts back and forth through work, inserting the needle where the yarn comes out.

Mane
Place mane across head behind ears and sew all edges of mane to head.

Tail
Join row-ends of tail and sew cast-on sts to first white stripe of body at centre back all the way round.

Zebras are extremely knowledgeable about blue and white Cornishware china and will answer almost any question on it.

The majority of a lion's time is taken up sleeping in trees or lying around in crazy poses. Lions are great climbers and hunters. Their eyesight is five times better than a human's and they can run the length of a football field in just six seconds.

LION

What you'll need

Measurement
Lion measures 9½in (24cm) in height

Materials
Any DK yarn:
100g golden-yellow (A)
50g burnt-orange (B)
50g brown (C)
Oddment of black for features
Note: amounts are generous but
approximate
A pair of 3.25mm (US3:UK10) needles
Acrylic toy stuffing
Plastic-headed marker pins

Tension
26 sts x 34 rows measure 4in (10cm) square
over stocking-st using 3.25mm needles
before stuffing

Abbreviations
See page 124

DID YOU KNOW? Lions make an art out of sleeping; sometimes they are only up for three hours a day.

How to make Lion

Body (make 2 pieces)

Beg at lower edge using the thumb method and A, cast on 35 sts.

First and next 4 foll alt rows: P.
Inc row: K10, m1, k15, m1, k10 (37 sts).
Inc row: K11, m1, k15, m1, k11 (39 sts).
Inc row: K12, m1, k15, m1, k12 (41 sts).
Inc row: K13, m1, k15, m1, k13 (43 sts).
Inc row: K14, m1, k15, m1, k14 (45 sts).
Beg with a p row, stocking-st 15 rows.
Dec row: K2tog, k to last 2 sts, k2tog tbl.
Next row: P.
Rep last 2 rows 12 more times (19 sts).
Cast off.

Base

Using the thumb method and A, cast on 20 sts.
First row: P.
Inc row: K1, m1, k to last st, m1, k1.
Rep first 2 rows 5 more times (32 sts).
Beg with a p row, stocking-st 5 rows.
Dec row: K2tog, k to last 2 sts, k2tog tbl.
Next row: P.
Rep last 2 rows 5 more times (20 sts).
Cast off.

Head

Beg at lower edge using the thumb method and A, cast on 9 sts.
First and next 5 foll alt rows: P.
Inc row: (Inc) to end (18 sts).
Inc row: (K1, inc) to end (27 sts).
Inc row: (K2, inc) to end (36 sts).
Inc row: (K3, inc) to end (45 sts).
Inc row: (K4, inc) to end (54 sts).
Inc row: (K5, inc) to end (63 sts).
Beg with a p row, stocking-st 19 rows.
Shape top of head
Dec row: (K5, k2tog) to end (54 sts).
Next and next 4 foll alt rows: P.
Dec row: (K4, k2tog) to end (45 sts).
Dec row: (K3, k2tog) to end (36 sts).
Dec row: (K2, k2tog) to end (28 sts).
Dec row: (K1, k2tog) to end (18 sts).

Dec row: (K2tog) to end (9 sts).
Thread yarn through rem sts, pull tight and secure.

Snout

First piece

Using the thumb method and A, cast on 12 sts.
Beg with a p row, stocking-st 3 rows.
Dec row: K1, k2tog, k to last 3 sts, k2tog tbl, k1.
Next row: P.
Rep last 2 rows 2 more times (6 sts).
Dec row: K1, k2tog, k2tog tbl, k1 (4 sts).
Thread yarn through rem sts, pull tight and secure.

Second piece

Using the thumb method and B, cast on 24 sts.
Beg with a p row, stocking-st 3 rows.
Dec row: (K1, k2tog, k6, k2tog tbl, k1) twice (20 sts).
Next and next 2 foll alt rows: P.
Dec row: (K1, k2tog, k4, k2tog tbl, k1) twice (16 sts).
Dec row: (K1, k2tog, k2, k2tog tbl, k1) twice (12 sts).
Dec row: (K1, k2tog, k2tog tbl, k1) twice (8 sts).
Thread yarn through rem sts and secure.

Hind legs (make 2)

Using the thumb method and A, cast on 32 sts.
Beg with a p row, stocking-st 13 rows.
Change to B.
Garter-st 10 rows.
Dec row: (K2, k2tog) to end (24 sts).
Garter-st 3 rows.
Dec row: (K1, k2tog) to end (16 sts).
K 1 row.
Dec row: (K2tog) to end (8 sts).
Thread yarn through rem sts, pull tight and secure.

Forelegs (make 2)

Using the thumb method and A, cast on 12 sts).
First row: Inc p-wise into every st (24 sts).
Stocking-st 26 rows.
Change to B.
Garter-st 8 rows.
Dec row: (K1, k2tog) to end (16 sts).
Garter-st 3 rows.
Dec row: (K2tog) to end (8 sts).
Thread yarn through rem sts, pull tight and secure.

Mane

Special abbreviation: loop-st
Insert RH needle into next st, place first finger of LH behind LH needle and wind yarn round needle and finger twice, then just round needle once. Knit st, pulling 3 loops through. Place these loops on LH needle and knit into the back of them. Pull loops sharply down to secure. Cont to next st.
Beg under chin using C, cast on 4 sts loosely.
Row 1: K1, (loop-st) to last st, k1.
Row 2: K.
Rows 3–7: Rep rows 1 and 2 twice, then row 1 again.
Row 8: K1, (inc) twice, k1 (6 sts).
Row 9: K1, (loop-st) to last st, k1.

Row 10: K.

Rows 11–15: Rep rows 9 and 10 twice, then row 9 again.

Row 16: K1, inc, k to last 2 sts, inc, k1.

Row 17: K1, (loop-st) to last st, k1.

Rows 18–25: Rep rows 16 and 17 4 times (16 sts).

Row 26: K.

Row 27: K1, (loop-st) to last st, k1.

Rows 28–51: Rep rows 26 and 27 12 times.

Row 52: K1, k2tog, k to last 2 sts, k2tog, k1.

Row 53: K1, (loop-st) to last st, k1.

Rows 54–61: Rep rows 52 and 53 4 times (6 sts).

Row 62: K.

Row 63: K1, (loop-st) to last st, k1.

Rows 64–67: Rep rows 62 and 63 twice.

Row 68: K1, (k2tog) twice, k1 (4 sts).

Row 69: K1, (loop-st) to last st, k1.

Row 70: K.

Rows 71–75: Rep rows 69 and 70 twice, then row 69 again.

Cast off.

Nose

Using the thumb method and black, cast on 6 sts.

P 1 row.

Dec row: K1, (k2tog) twice, k1 (4 sts).

Dec row: P1, p2tog, p1 (3 sts).

Thread yarn through rem sts, pull tight and secure.

Ears (make 2)

Beg at lower edge using the thumb method and A, cast on 8 sts.

P 1 row.

Inc row: K1, (m1, k1) to end (15 sts).

Beg with a p row, stocking-st 5 rows.

Dec row: (K1, k2tog) to end (10 sts).

Thread yarn through rem sts, pull tight and secure.

Tail

Using the thumb method and A, cast on 16 sts.

Beg with a p row, stocking-st 11 rows.

Change to B.

Garter-st 8 rows.

Dec row: (K2tog) to end (8 sts).

Thread yarn through rem sts, pull tight and secure.

Making up

Body

Place two halves of body together matching all edges and join row-ends. Stuff body leaving neck and lower edge open.

Base

Pin base to lower edge of body and sew base to body all the way round, adding more stuffing to base if needed.

Head

Gather round cast-on sts of head, pull tight and secure. Join row-ends of head leaving gap, stuff and close gap. Pin head to body, adding more stuffing to neck if needed. Sew in place by taking a small horizontal st from head and then a small horizontal st from body and doing this alternately all the way round.

Snout

Place right sides of snout pieces together matching sts pulled tight on a thread of both pieces. Join row-ends by sewing back and forth 1 st in from edge. Turn right-side out and stuff. Sew snout to centre front of head, sewing lower edge of snout to neck.

Hind legs

Join row-ends of legs, leaving cast-on sts open, and stuff. Place body on a flat surface and pin and sew legs to body all the way round.

Forelegs

Join row-ends of forelegs and stuff. With seam at centre of inside edge, over-sew cast-on sts. Sew cast-on sts of each foreleg to either side of neck, and inside edge of forelegs to body.

Mane

Place mane on head joining under chin. Sew all edges down.

Nose

Place nose on snout and sew all edges down.

Ears

Join row-ends of ears. With seam at centre back, part the mane and sew ears to head.

Tail

Join row-ends of tail. Stuff tail and sew to back of lion.

Embroidering the features

Embroider mouth in black as shown in picture. To begin and fasten off invisibly for the embroidery, tie a knot in end of yarn and take a large st through work, coming up to start the embroidery. Allow knot to disappear through knitting and be caught in stuffing. To fasten off, take a few sts back and forth through work, inserting needle where yarn comes out. To make eyes, tie a knot in 2 lengths of black yarn winding the yarn round 6 times to make each knot (see page 122). Check that the knots are the same size. Tie eyes to 5th row above snout with 7 clear knitted sts in between. Run ends into head.

Giant pandas are native to China where they are called 'large bear-cats'.
They spend at least 12 hours a day eating bamboo and will consume as much
as 84lbs (38kg) of it. Although giant pandas seem pretty quiet, they bleat,
roar, growl, honk, croak and squeal.

GIANT PANDA

What you'll need

Measurement
Giant panda measures 9½in (24cm)
in height

Materials
Any DK yarn:
100g white (A)
100g black (B)
25g biscuit (C)
25g green (D)
*Note: amounts are generous but
approximate*
A pair of 3.25mm (US3:UK10) needles
Acrylic toy stuffing
Plastic-headed marker pins
Plastic drinking straw

Tension
26 sts x 34 rows measure 4in (10cm) square
over stocking-st using 3.25mm needles
before stuffing

Abbreviations
See page 124

How to make Giant Panda

Body (make 2 pieces)

Beg at lower edge using the thumb method and A, cast on 35 sts.

First and next 4 foll alt rows: P.

Inc row: K10, m1, k15, m1, k10 (37 sts).

Inc row: K11, m1, k15, m1, k11 (39 sts).

Inc row: K12, m1, k15, m1, k12 (41 sts).

Inc row: K13, m1, k15, m1, k13 (43 sts).

Inc row: K14, m1, k15, m1, k14 (45 sts).

Beg with a p row, stocking-st 17 rows.

Dec row: K2tog, k to last 2 sts, k2tog tbl.

P 1 row.

Change to B.

Dec row: K2tog, k to last 2 sts, k2tog tbl.

Next row: P.

Rep last 2 rows 8 more times (25 sts).

Cast off.

Base

Using the thumb method and A, cast on 20 sts.

First row: P.

Inc row: K1, m1, k to last st, m1, k1.

Rep first 2 rows 5 more times (32 sts).

Beg with a p row, stocking-st 5 rows.

Dec row: K2tog, k to last 2 sts, k2tog tbl.

Next row: P.

Rep last 2 rows 5 more times (20 sts).

Cast off.

Head

Beg at lower edge using the thumb method and A, cast on 10 sts.

First and next 6 foll alt rows: P.

Inc row: (Inc) to end (20 sts).

Inc row: (K1, inc) to end (30 sts).

Inc row: (K2, inc) to end (40 sts).

Inc row: (K3, inc) to end (50 sts).

Inc row: (K4, inc) to end (60 sts).

Inc row: (K5, inc) to end (70 sts).

Inc row: (K6, inc) to end (80 sts).

Beg with a p row, stocking-st 15 rows.

DID YOU KNOW? Pandas are shy and generally solitary creatures, only meeting up with other pandas occasionally.

Shape head

Dec row: (K8, k2tog) to end (72 sts).

Beg with a p row, stocking-st 3 rows.

Dec row: (K7, k2tog) to end (64 sts).

Beg with a p row, stocking-st 3 rows.

Dec row: (K6, k2tog) to end (56 sts).

Next and next 5 foll alt rows: P.

Dec row: (K5, k2tog) to end (48 sts).

Dec row: (K4, k2tog) to end (40 sts).

Dec row: (K3, k2tog) to end (32 sts).

Dec row: (K2, k2tog) to end (24 sts).

Dec row: (K1, k2tog) to end (16 sts).

Dec row: (K2tog) to end (8 sts).

Thread yarn through rem sts, pull tight and secure.

Hind legs (make 2)

Note: follow individual instructions for right and left legs.

Beg at sole using the thumb method and B, cast on 22 sts.

Place a marker at centre of cast-on sts.

P 1 row.

Inc row: K1, (m1, k1) to end (43 sts).

Beg with a p row, stocking-st 15 rows.

Dec for right leg: K4, (k2tog) 10 times, k19 (33 sts).

Dec for left leg: K19, (k2tog) 10 times, k4 (33 sts).

Beg with a p row, stocking-st 5 rows.

Cast off 9 sts at beg of next 2 rows (15 sts).

Dec row: (K2tog) twice, k to last 4 sts, k2tog, k2tog tbl (11 sts).

Dec row: P2tog tbl, p to last 2 sts, p2tog (9 sts). Cast off.

Arms (make 2)

Beg at shoulder using the thumb method and B, cast on 8 sts.

First and next foll alt row: P.

Inc row: (Inc) to end (16 sts).

Inc row: (K1, inc) to end (24 sts).

Beg with a p row, stocking-st 15 rows.

Shape elbow

Row 1: K4, turn.

Row 2: S1p, p to end.

Row 3: K6, turn.

Row 4: S1p, p to end.

Row 5: K8, turn.

Row 6: S1p, p to end.

Row 7: K10, turn.

Row 8: S1p, p to end.

Next row: K across all sts.

Shape second half of elbow

Row 1: P4, turn.

Row 2: S1k, k to end.

Row 3: P6, turn.

Row 4: S1k, k to end.

Row 5: P8, turn.

Row 6: S1k, k to end.

Row 7: P10, turn.

Row 8: S1k, k to end.

Next row: P across all sts.

Stocking-st 10 rows.

Dec row: (K1, k2tog) to end (16 sts).

P 1 row.

Dec row: (k2tog) to end (8 sts).

Thread yarn through rem sts, pull tight and secure.

Snout

Using the thumb method and A, cast on 30 sts.

Beg with a p row, stocking-st 3 rows.

Dec row: K2tog, k6, (k2tog) twice, k6, (k2tog) twice, k6, k2tog tbl (24 sts).

Next and next foll alt row: P.

Dec row: K2tog, k4, (k2tog) twice, k4, (k2tog) twice, k4, k2tog tbl (18 sts).

Dec row: K2tog, k2, (k2tog) twice, k2,

(k2tog) twice, k2, k2tog tbl (12 sts).

P 1 row.

Thread yarn through sts, pull tight and secure.

Nose

Using the thumb method and B, cast on 6 sts.

P 1 row.

Dec row: K1, (k2tog) twice, k1 (4 sts).

Dec row: P1, p2tog, p1 (3 sts).

Thread yarn through rem sts, pull tight and secure.

Eye patches (make 2)

Note: eye patches are worked in garter-st.

Using the thumb method and B, cast on 6 sts.

Garter-st 12 rows.

Dec row: K2tog, k to last 2 sts, k2tog tbl (4 sts).

Dec row: K1, k2tog, k1 (3 sts).

Thread yarn through rem sts, pull tight and secure.

Ears (make 2)

Using the thumb method and B, cast on 16 sts.

P 1 row.

Inc row: K1, (m1, k2) to last st, m1, k1 (24 sts).

Beg with a p row, stocking-st 7 rows.

Dec row: (K2, k2tog) to end (18 sts).

P 1 row.

Dec row: (K1, k2tog) to end (12 sts).

Dec row: (P2tog) to end (6 sts).

Thread yarn through rem sts, pull tight and secure.

Tail

Using the thumb method and A, cast on 10 sts.

P 1 row.

Inc row: K2, (m1, k2) to end (14 sts).

Next row: P.

Inc row: K1, m1, k to last st, m1, k1.

Rep last 2 rows once (18 sts).

P 1 row.

Cast on 3 sts at beg of next 2 rows, working the 4th st of each row tbl (24 sts).

Stocking-st 6 rows.

Dec row: (K1, k2tog) to end (16 sts).

P 1 row.

Dec row: (K2tog) to end (8 sts).

Thread yarn through rem sts, pull tight and secure.

Bamboo

Beg at lower edge using the thumb method and C, cast on 4 sts.

Inc row: Inc k-wise into each st (8 sts).

K 1 row.

Beg with a k row, work in stocking-st for 2in (5cm), ending on a p row.

Garter-st 4 rows.

Beg with a k row, work in stocking-st for 3¼in (8cm), ending on a p row.

Garter-st 2 rows.

Dec row: (K2tog) to end (4 sts).

Thread yarn through rem sts, pull tight and secure.

Leaves (make 6 pieces)

Using the thumb method and D, cast on 1 st.

Inc row: (K1, p1, k1) into first st (3 sts).

P 1 row.

Inc row: K1, m1, k1, m1, k1 (5 sts).

Beg with a p row, stocking-st 9 rows.

Dec row: K2tog, k1, k2tog tbl (3 sts).

Beg with a p row, stocking-st 3 rows.

Dec row: K3tog tbl (1 st).

Fasten off.

giant panda

Making up

Body
Place the two halves of body together matching all edges and join row-ends. Stuff body leaving neck and lower edge open.

Base
Pin base to lower edge of body and sew base to body all the way round, adding more stuffing to base if needed.

Head
Gather round cast-on sts of head, pull tight and secure. Join row-ends of head leaving gap, stuff and close gap. Pin head to body adding more stuffing to neck if needed. Sew in place using black yarn by taking a small horizontal st from head and then a small horizontal st from body and doing this alternately all the way round.

Hind legs
Join row-ends of hind legs and bring marker and seam together, over-sew cast-on sts. Stuff legs, pushing stuffing into toes. Stand body on flat surface and pin legs to body. Sew legs to body all the way round.

Arms
Gather round cast-on sts at shoulder, pull tight and secure. Join row-ends of arms leaving gap, stuff and close gap. Sew arms to body at each side.

Snout
Join row-ends of snout and stuff. Pin and sew snout to face.

Nose
Place nose onto the snout and then sew all edges down.

Ears
Join row-ends of ears and with seam at centre back, sew ears to head.

Tail
Join row-ends of tail from sts on a thread to cast-off sts. Stuff and sew to back of panda.

Eye patches
Sew eye patches to face around snout.

Embroidering the features
Embroider a circle of white for each eye using chain-stitch. Embroider mouth in black as in picture. To begin and fasten off invisibly for the embroidery, tie a knot in end of yarn and take a large st through work, coming up to start the embroidery. Allow knot to disappear through knitting and be caught in stuffing. To fasten off, take a few sts back and forth through work, inserting needle where yarn comes out.

Bamboo
Gather round cast-on sts of bamboo, pull tight and secure. Cut an extra wide drinking straw to 6¼in (16cm) and enclose straw in knitting by joining row-ends of bamboo around it.

Leaves
Make 3 leaves by placing wrong sides of 2 pieces together, matching all edges and sew around edge. Sew leaves to bamboo as in picture.

DID YOU KNOW? Pandas are pink when they are born. The black markings develop after about a month.

In many cultures the tiger is a symbol of strength and courage. They are the largest of the big cats with night vision six times greater than a human's. The pattern of their stripes is like the human fingerprint, unique to each individual.

TIGER

Tigers, like most cats, enjoy a good rest.

What you'll need

Measurement
Tiger measures 9½in (24cm) in height

Materials
Any DK yarn:
100g orange (A)
50g black (B)
20g cream (C)
Oddment of grey for features

Note: amounts are generous but approximate
A pair of 3.25mm (US3:UK10) needles
Acrylic toy stuffing
Plastic-headed marker pins

Tension
26 sts x 34 rows measure 4in (10cm) square
over stocking-st using 3.25mm needles
before stuffing

Abbreviations
See page124

Pattern notes
Before beginning to knit, wind yarns
A and B into two separate balls

Tigers are shy.

How to make Tiger

Body (make 2 pieces)
Note: 2 separate balls of A are required.
Beg at lower edge using the thumb method and first ball of A, cast on 35 sts.
P 1 row.
Join in B and second ball of A and work in stocking-st in stripe, carrying yarn loosely up sides of work.
Row 1: Using A, k10, m1, k15, m1, k10 (37 sts).
Row 2: Using A, p.
Row 3: Using B, k11, m1, k15, m1, k11 (39 sts).
Row 4: Using A (second ball), p.
Row 5: Using A, k12, m1, k15, m1, k12 (41 sts).
Row 6: Using B, p.
Row 7: Using A, k13, m1, k15, m1, k13 (43 sts).
Row 8: Using A, p.
Row 9: Using A, k14, m1, k15, m1, k14 (45 sts).
Row 10: Using A, p.
Row 11: Using B, k.
Rows 12 and 13: Using A, stocking-st 2 rows.
Row 14: Using B, p.
Rows 15–18: Using A, stocking-st 4 rows.
Row 19: Using B, k.
Rows 20 and 21: Using A, stocking-st 2 rows.
Row 22: Using B, p.

Shape sides
Row 23: Using A, k2tog, k to last 2 sts, k2tog tbl (43 sts).
Row 24: Using A, p.
Row 25: Using A, k2tog, k to last 2 sts, k2tog tbl (41 sts).
Row 26: Using A, p.
Cont in stripe as set for 22 more rows, dec 1 st at each end of next and every foll alt row (19 sts).
Cast off in A.

Base
Using the thumb method and A, cast on 20 sts.
First row: P.
Inc row: K1, m1, k to last st, m1, k1.
Rep first 2 rows 5 more times (32 sts).
Beg with a p row, stocking-st 5 rows.
Dec row: K2tog, k to last 2 sts, k2tog tbl.
Next row: P.
Rep last 2 rows 5 more times (20 sts).
Cast off.

Head
Note: 2 separate balls of A are required.
Beg at centre back using the thumb method and first ball of A, cast on 8 sts.
P 1 row.

Join on B and second ball of A and work in stocking-st in stripe, carrying yarn loosely up sides of work.
Row 1: Using A, k1, (m1, k1) to end (15 sts).
Row 2: Using A, p.
Row 3: Using B, k1, (m1, k2) to end (22 sts).
Row 4: Using A (second ball), p.
Row 5: Using A, k1, (m1, k3) to end (29 sts).
Row 6: Using B, p.
Row 7: Using A, k1, (m1, k4) to end (38 sts).
Row 8: Using A, p.
Row 9: Using A, k1, (m1, k5) to end (43 sts).
Row 10: Using A, p.
Row 11: Using B, k1, (m1, k6) to end (50 sts).
Row 12: Using A, p.
Row 13: Using A, k1, (m1, k7) to end (57 sts).
Row 14: Using B, p.
Row 15: Using A, k1, (m1, k8) to end (64 sts).
Keeping stripe patt correct and beg with a p row, stocking-st 23 rows, ending with 10th black stripe.
Cont with 1 ball of A.

Shape face
Dec row: Using A, (k6, k2tog) to end (56 sts).
Next row: Using A, p.
Dec row: Using A, (k5, k2tog) to end (48 sts).
Next row: Using A, p.
Dec row: Using B, (k4, k2tog) to end (40 sts).
Next row: Using A, p.
Dec row: Using A, (k3, k2tog) to end (32 sts).
Next row: Using B, p.
Cont with 1 ball of A.
Dec row: (K2, k2tog) to end (24 sts).
Next row and next foll alt row: P.
Dec row: (K1, k2tog) to end (16 sts).
Dec row: (K2tog) to end (8 sts).
Thread yarn through rem sts, pull tight and secure.

Snout
First piece
Using the thumb method and A, cast on 12 sts.

Beg with a p row, stocking-st 3 rows.

Dec row: K1, k2tog, k to last 3 sts, k2tog tbl, k1.

Next row: P.

Rep last 2 rows twice more (6 sts).

Dec row: K1, k2tog, k2tog tbl, k1 (4 sts).

Thread yarn through rem sts, pull tight and secure.

Second piece
Using the thumb method and C, cast on 24 sts.

Beg with a p row, stocking-st 3 rows.

Dec row: (K1, k2tog, k6, k2tog tbl, k1) twice (20 sts).

Next and next 2 foll alt rows: P.

Dec row: (K1, k2tog, k4, k2tog tbl, k1) twice (16 sts).

Dec row: (K1, k2tog, k2, k2tog tbl, k1) twice (12 sts).

Dec row: (K1, k2tog, k2tog tbl, k1) twice (8 sts).

Thread yarn through rem sts, pull tight and secure.

Hind legs (make 2)
Note: 2 separate balls of A are required.
Using the thumb method and A, cast on 40 sts.

P 1 row.

Join on B and second ball of A and work in stocking-st in stripe, carrying yarn loosely up sides of work.

Row 1: Using B, k.

Rows 2 and 3: Using A (second ball) work in stocking-st, beg with a p row.

Row 4: Using B, p.

Rows 5–8: Using A, stocking-st 4 rows.

Rows 9–16: As rows 1–8.

Cont in B.

Stocking-st 4 rows.

Dec row: (K3, k2tog) to end (32 sts).

Next and next 2 foll alt rows: P.

Dec row: (K2, k2tog) to end (24 sts).

Dec row: (K1, k2tog) to end (16 sts).

Dec row: (K2tog) to end (8 sts).

Thread yarn through rem sts, pull tight and secure.

Forelegs (make 2)
Note: 2 separate balls of A are required.
Using the thumb method and A, cast on 15 sts.

Row 1: Inc p-wise into every st (30 sts).

Join in B and second ball of A and work in stocking-st in stripe, carrying yarn loosely up sides of work.

Stripe pattern
Row 1: Using B, k.

Rows 2 and 3: Using A (second ball), beg with a p row, stocking-st 2 rows.

Row 4: Using B, p.

Rows 5–8: Using A, stocking-st 4 rows.

Rows 9–24: As rows 1–8 twice.

Using B, stocking-st 6 rows.

Dec row: (K1, k2tog) to end (20 sts).

P 1 row.

Dec row: (K2tog) to end (10 sts).

Dec row: (P2tog) to end (5 sts).

Thread yarn through rem sts, pull tight and secure.

Nose
Using the thumb method and B, cast on 6 sts.

P 1 row.

Dec row: K1, (k2tog) twice, k1 (4 sts).

Dec row: P1, p2tog, p1 (3 sts).

Thread yarn through rem sts, pull tight and secure.

Ears (make 2)
First piece
Note: 2 separate balls of B are required.
Beg at lower edge using the thumb method and A and B, cast on 3 sts inB, 6 sts in A and 3 sts in B (second ball), all on the same needle (12 sts).

Work in blocks of colour using a separate ball of yarn for each block and twisting when changing yarn.

First row: P3-B, p6-A, p3-B.

Next row: K3-B, k6-A, k3-B.

Rep first row once.

Dec row: K3-B, k2tog, k2, k2tog tbl-A, k3-B (10 sts).

Next row: P3-B, p4-A, p3-B.

Dec row: K3-B, k2tog, k2tog tbl-A, k3-B (8 sts).

Next row: P3-B, p2-A, p3-B.

Cont with 1 ball of B.

Dec row: K3, k2tog, k3 (7 sts).

Dec row: P2, p3tog, p2 (5 sts).

Dec row: K1, k3tog, k1 (3 sts).

Thread yarn through rem sts, pull tight and secure.

Second piece
Beg at lower edge using B, cast on 11 sts.

Beg with a p row stocking-st 3 rows.

Dec row: K1, k2tog, k to last 3 sts, k2tog tbl, k1.

Next row: P.

Rep last 2 rows twice more (5 sts).

Dec row: K1, k3tog, k1 (3 sts).

Thread yarn through rem sts, pull tight and secure.

tiger

Tail

Note: 2 separate balls of A are required. Using the thumb method and first ball of A, cast on 18 sts.

P 1 row.

Join in B and second ball of A and work in stocking-st in stripe, carrying yarn loosely up sides of work.

Rows 1 and 2: Using A, beg with a k row, stocking-st 2 rows.

Row 3: Using B, k.

Rows 4 and 5: Using A (second ball), stocking-st 2 rows beg with a p row.

Row 6: Using B, p.

Row 7: Using A, k.

Row 8: Using A, p8, turn.

Row 9: Using A, s1k, k to end.

Row 10: Using A, p.

Row 11: Using A, k8, turn.

Row 12: Using A, s1p, p to end.

Row 13: Using B, k.

Row 14 and 15: Using A, beg with a p row, stocking-st 2 rows.

Row 16: Using B, p.

Rows 17–26: As rows 7–16 once.

Cont with 1 ball of A.

Next and next foll alt row: K.

Dec row: (P1, p2tog) to end (12 sts).

Dec row: (P2tog) to end (6 sts). Thread yarn through rem sts, pull tight and secure.

Making up

Body

Place two halves of body together matching all edges and join row-ends by sewing back and forth 1 st in from edge. Stuff body leaving neck and lower edge open.

Base

Pin base to lower edge of body and sew base to body all the way round, adding more stuffing to base if needed.

Head

Gather round cast-on sts of head, pull tight and secure. Join row-ends of head leaving gap, stuff and close gap. Pin head to body, adding more stuffing to neck if needed. With sts pulled tight on a thread at centre front and cast-on sts at centre back, sew in place by taking a small horizontal st from head and then a small horizontal st from body and doing this alternately all the way round.

Snout

Place right sides of both pieces of snout together matching sts pulled tight on a thread of both pieces. Join row-ends by sewing back and forth 1 st in from edge. Turn right-side out and stuff. Sew snout to lower half of head at centre front.

Hind legs

Join row-ends of hind legs on wrong side by sewing back and forth 1 st in from edge. Leaving cast-on sts open, stuff. Place body on a flat surface and pin and sew legs to body all the way round.

Forelegs

Join row-ends of forelegs on wrong side by sewing back and forth 1 st in from edge. Stuff, and with seam at centre of inside edge, over-sew cast-on sts. Sew cast-on sts of each foreleg to neck either side of body, and inside edge of forelegs to halfway down body.

Nose

Place nose on snout and sew all edges down.

Ears

Place right sides of first and second ear pieces together and join row-ends by sewing back and forth 1 st in from edge. Turn right-side out and sew lower edges of ears to head.

Tail

Join row-ends of tail from sts on a thread to cast-off sts, by sewing back and forth 1 s in from edge. Leaving cast-on sts open, stuf and, with tip of tail curling upwards, sew to back of tiger with seam underneath.

Embroidering the features

Embroider mouth in black as shown. To begin and fasten off invisibly for the embroidery, tie a knot in end of yarn and take a large st through work, coming up to start the embroidery. Allow knot to disappear through knitting and be caught in stuffing. To fasten off, take a few sts back and forth through work, inserting needle where yarn comes out. To make eyes, tie a knot in 2 lengths of grey yarn, winding the yarn round 6 times to make each knot (see page 122). Check that the knots are the same size. Tie eyes to 5th row above snout with 8 clear knitted sts in between. Run ends into head.

Happy tiger: He's right at the top of the food chain.

Crocodiles are most at home in or near the water. They can swim up to 20mph (32kph) and hold their breath underwater for more than an hour. They are very fast over short distances, even out of water, and can reach speeds of 11mph (17.6kph) when they 'belly run'. Crocodiles als have exceptional hearing. They can even hear their young calling from inside their eggshells!

CROCODILE

What you'll need

Measurement
Crocodile measures 19in (48cm) from
head to tail

Materials
Any DK yarn:
100g green (A)
20g white (B)
20g black (C)
Note: amounts are generous
but approximate
A pair of 3.25mm (US3:UK10) needles
Acrylic toy stuffing
Plastic-headed marker pins

Tension
26 sts x 34 rows measure 4in (10cm) square
over stocking-st using 3.25mm needles
before stuffing

Abbreviations
See page 124
Special abbreviation: Moss-st
Beg with a k st, k1, (p1, k1) to end
This row is repeated

DID YOU KNOW? A crocodile
cannot stick its tongue out,
however much it may want to.

crocodile

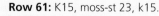

How to make Crocodile

Body and head

Beg at tail using the thumb method and A, cast on 7 sts.

P 1 row.

Row 1: K1, (m1, k1) to end (13 sts).
Row 2: P5, moss-st 3, p5.
Row 3: K3, moss-st 7, k3.
Row 4: As row 2.
Row 5: K3, (m1, k1) twice, moss-st 3, (m1, k1) twice, k3 (17 sts).
Row 6: P5, moss-st 7, p5.
Row 7: K5, moss-st 7, k5.
Row 8: As row 6.
Row 9: As row 7.
Row 10: As row 6.
Row 11: K3, (m1, k1) twice, moss-st 7, (m1, k1) twice, k3 (21 sts).
Row 12: P7, moss-st 7, p7.
Row 13: K7, moss-st 7, k7.
Row 14: As row 12.
Row 15: As row 13.
Row 16: As row 12.
Row 17: K5, (m1, k1) twice, moss-st 7, (m1, k1) twice, k5 (25 sts).
Row 18: P7, moss-st 11, p7.
Row 19: K7, moss-st 11, k7.
Row 20: As row 18.
Row 21: As row 19.
Row 22: As row 18.
Row 23: K5, (m1, k1) twice, moss-st 11, (m1, k1) twice, k5 (29 sts).
Row 24: P9, moss-st 11, p9.
Row 25: K9, moss-st 11, k9.
Row 26: As row 24.
Row 27: As row 25.
Row 28: As row 24.
Row 29: K7, (m1, k1) twice, moss-st 11, (m1, k1) twice, k7 (33 sts).
Row 30: P9, moss-st 15, p9.
Row 31: K9, moss-st 15, k9.

Row 32: As row 30.
Row 33: As row 31.
Row 34: As row 30.
Row 35: K7, (m1, k1) twice, moss-st 15, (m1, k1) twice, k7 (37 sts).
Row 36: P11, moss-st 15, p11.
Row 37: K11, moss-st 15, k11.
Row 38: As row 36.
Row 39: As row 37.
Row 40: As row 36.
Row 41: K9, (m1, k1) twice, moss-st 15, (m1, k1) twice, k9 (41 sts).
Row 42: P11, moss-st 19, p11.
Row 43: K11, moss-st 19, k11.
Row 44: As row 42.
Row 45: As row 43.
Row 46: As row 42.
Row 47: K9, (m1, k1) twice, moss-st 19, (m1, k1) twice, k9 (45 sts).
Row 48: P13, moss-st 19, p13.
Row 49: K13, moss-st 19, k13.
Row 50: As row 48.
Row 51: As row 49.
Row 52: As row 48.
Row 53: K11, (m1, k1) twice, moss-st 19, (m1, k1) twice, k11 (49 sts).
Row 54: P13, moss-st 23, p13.
Row 55: K13, moss-st 23, k13.
Row 56: As row 54.
Row 57: As row 55.
Row 58: As row 54.
Row 59: K11, (m1, k1) twice, moss-st 23, (m1, k1) twice, k11 (53 sts).
Row 60: P15, moss-st 23, p15.

Row 61: K15, moss-st 23, k15.
Row 62: As row 60.
Row 63: As row 61.
Row 64: As row 60.
Row 65: K13, (m1, k1) twice, moss-st 23, (m1, k1) twice, k13 (57 sts).
Row 66: P15, moss-st 27, p15.
Row 67: K15, moss-st 27, k15.
Row 68: As row 66.
Row 69: As row 67.
Row 70: As row 66.
Row 71: K13, (m1, k1) twice, moss-st 27, (m1, k1) twice, k13 (61 sts).
Row 72: P17, moss-st 27, p17.
Row 73: K17, moss-st 27, k17.
Row 74: As row 72.
Row 75: As row 73.
Row 76: As row 72.
Row 77: K15, (m1, k1) twice, moss-st 27, (m1, k1) twice, k15 (65 sts).
Row 78: P17, moss-st 31, p17.
Row 79: K17, moss-st 31, k17.
Row 80: P17, moss-st 31, k17.
Rep rows 79 and 80 30 more times.
Dec row: K16, k3tog tbl, moss-st 27, k3tog, k16 (61 sts).
Next row: P17, moss-st 27, p17.
Next row: K17, moss-st 27, k17.
Next row: P17, moss-st 27, p17.
Dec row: K16, k3tog tbl, moss-st 23, k3tog, k16 (57 sts).
Next row: P17, moss-st 23, p17.
Next row: K17, moss-st 23, k17.
Next row: P17, moss-st 23, p17.
Dec row: K16, k3tog tbl, moss-st 19, k3tog, k16 (53 sts).
Next row: P17, moss-st 19, p17.
Next row: K17, moss-st 19, k17.
Next row: P17, moss-st 19, p17.
Dec row: K16, k3tog tbl, moss-st 15, k3tog, k16 (49 sts).
Beg with a p row, stocking-st 21 rows.
Dec row: K7, (k3, k2tog) 7 times, k7 (42 sts).
P 1 row.

Dec row: K7, (k2, k2tog) 7 times, k7 (35 sts).
Beg with a p row, stocking-st 3 rows.
Dec row: K7, (k1, k2tog) 7 times, k7 (28 sts).
Beg with a p row, stocking-st 19 rows.
Dec row: (K2, k2tog) to end (21 sts).
P 1 row.
Dec row: (K1, k2tog) to end (14 sts).
Dec row: (P2tog) to end (7 sts).

Legs (make 4)
Beg at lower edge using the thumb method and A, cast on 14 sts.
Inc row: (K1, inc) to end (21 sts).
Cont in moss-st.
Moss-st 7 rows.
Shape gusset
Dec row: K2tog, moss-st to last 2 sts, k2tog tbl.
Dec row: K1, p2tog, moss-st to last 3 sts, p2tog, k1.
Moss-st 2 rows.
Rep last 4 rows once (13 sts).
Inc row: K1, inc k-wise into next st, moss-st to last 2 sts, inc k-wise, k1.
Inc row: Inc k-wise into first st, moss-st to last st, inc k-wise.
Moss-st 2 rows.
Rep last 4 rows once (21 sts).
Moss-st 6 rows.
Dec row: K1, (p3tog, k1) to end (11 sts).
Moss-st 1 row.
Thread yarn through sts, pull tight and secure.

Feet (make 8 pieces)
Note: feet are worked in garter-st.
Using the thumb method and A, cast on 18 sts.
Row 1: K.
Row 2: K6 turn.
Row 3: S1k, k to end.
Row 4: Cast off 5 sts at beg of next row (13 sts).
Row 5: K.

Row 6: Cast on 5 sts at beg of next row and k the 6th st of row tbl (18 sts).
Rep rows 1–6 once.
Next row: K.
Next row: K6, turn.
Next row: S1k, k to end.
Cast off loosely in garter-st.

Eyes (make 2)
Using the thumb method and B, cast on 6 sts.
P 1 row.
Inc row: (Inc) to end (12 sts).
Beg with a p row, stocking-st 3 rows.
Change to C.
Stocking-st 3 rows, ending on a k row.
Thread yarn through sts, pull tight and secure.

Eyelids (make 2)
Using the thumb method and A, cast on 10 sts.
Beg with a p row, stocking-st 2 rows, ending on a k row.
Dec row: (P2tog) to end (5 sts).
Thread yarn through rem sts, pull tight and secure.

Making up
Body and head
Join row-ends of head and stuff. Join row-ends of body beginning at tail and stuff lightly as you go, keeping body flat.

Legs and feet
Join straight row-ends of legs above and below the gusset. Bring gusset together horizontally and over-sew. Stuff legs and fold cast-on sts in half and over-sew. Take 2 pieces of feet and place together, matching all edges. Over-sew edges, sewing cast-on and cast-off sts together and sew round toes.

Push a small amount of stuffing inside and gather straight row-ends, pull tight and then secure. Sew feet to lower edge of legs. Place crocodile on a flat surface and assemble legs. Sew legs to body.

Eyes
Join row-ends of eyes and gather round cast-on sts, pull tight and secure. Press eyes flat, like a button, and sew to head, with seam under eyelid.

Eyelids
Sew eyelids to head, overlapping eyes. Sew cast-on sts of lids to eyes.

Embroidering the features
Using black, embroider a curving mouth in chain-stitch. Embroider 2 long sts in black as nostrils at end of snout. Embroider teeth in white, taking uneven straight sts along mouth, starting and finishing invisibly for embroidery (see page 122).

crocodile

75

There are 125 different species of monkey. The loudest are howler monkeys, which can be heard more than 3 miles (5km) away. All monkeys love to eat bananas. Some species have cheek pouches, so they can stuff the fruit in on the run for later. Colobus monkeys also see burping as a friendly social gesture.

MONKEY

What you'll need

Measurement
Monkey measures 12½in (32cm) in height

Materials
Any DK yarn:
100g brown (A)
50g biscuit (B)
25g yellow (C)
25g cream (D)
Oddment of black for features
Note: amounts are generous but
approximate
A pair of 3.25mm (US3:UK10) needles
Acrylic toy stuffing
Plastic-headed marker pins
Tweezers for stuffing small parts (optional)

Tension
26 sts x 34 rows measure 4in (10cm) square
over stocking-st using 3.25mm needles
before stuffing

Abbreviations
See page 124

DID YOU KNOW? A monkey was once tried and convicted for smoking a cigarette in South Bend, Indiana, USA.

How to make Monkey

Body (make 2 pieces)
Beg at lower edge using the thumb method and A, cast on 24 sts.

First and next foll 3 alt rows: P.

Inc row: K5, m1, k14, m1, k5
(26 sts).

Inc row: K6, m1, k14, m1, k6
(28 sts).

Inc row: K7, m1, k14, m1, k7
(30 sts).

Inc row: K8, m1, k14, m1, k8
(32 sts).

Beg with a p row, stocking-st 19 rows.

Dec row: K2tog, k to last 2 sts, k2tog tbl.

Next row: P.

Rep last 2 rows 8 times more (14 sts).

Cast off.

Base
Using the thumb method and A, cast on 14 sts.

First row: P.

Inc row: K1, m1, k to last st, m1, k1.

Rep first 2 rows 2 more times (20 sts).

Beg with a p row, stocking-st 5 rows.

Dec row: K2tog, k to last 2 sts, k2tog tbl.

P 1 row.

Rep last 2 rows twice more (14 sts).

Cast off.

Head
Beg at lower edge using the thumb method and A, cast on 9 sts.

First and next 4 foll alt rows: P.

Inc row: (Inc) to end (18 sts).

Inc row: (K1, inc) to end (27 sts).

Inc row: (K2, inc) to end (36 sts).

Inc row: (K3, inc) to end (45 sts).

Inc row: (K4, inc) to end (54 sts).

Beg with a p row, stocking-st 17 rows.

Shape top of head
Dec row: (K4, k2tog) to end (45 sts).

Beg with a p row, stocking-st 3 rows.

Dec row: (K3, k2tog) to end (36 sts).

Next and next 2 foll alt rows: P.

Dec row: (K2, k2tog) to end (27 sts).

Dec row: (K1, k2tog) to end (18 sts).

Dec row: (K2tog) to end (9 sts).

Thread yarn through rem sts, pull tight and secure.

Muzzle
Using the thumb method and B, cast on 28 sts.

P 1 row.

Inc row: K1, (m1, k2) to last st, m1, k1
(44 sts).

Beg with a p row, stocking-st 3 rows.

Dec row: K2, (k2tog, k2) to end
(32 sts).

Beg with a p row, stocking-st 3 rows.

Dec row: K2, (k2tog) 6 times, k4, (k2tog)
6 times, k2, (20 sts).

P 1 row.

Cast off.

Eye piece
Beg at lower edge using the thumb method and B, cast on 12 sts.

P 1 row.

Inc row: K1, m1, k to last st, m1, k1
(14 sts).

Beg with a p row, stocking-st 3 rows.

Next row: K7.

Turn and work on these 7 sts.

P 1 row.

Dec row: K2tog, k to last 2 sts, k2tog tbl
(5 sts).

Dec row: P2tog tbl, p1, p2tog (3 sts).

Break yarn and thread through sts, pull tight and secure.

Rejoin yarn to rem sts and k 1 row (7 sts).

Complete to match first side.

Ears (make 2)
Using the thumb method and B, cast on 12 sts.

Beg with a p row, stocking-st 5 rows.

Dec row: (K2tog) to end (6 sts).

Thread yarn through rem sts, pull tight and secure.

Legs (make 2)
Using the thumb method and A, cast on 20 sts.

Beg with a p row, stocking-st 45 rows.

Cast off.

Feet (make 2)
Using the thumb method and B, cast on 18 sts.

P 1 row.

Inc row: K2, (m1, k2) to end (26 sts).

Beg with a p row, stocking-st 5 rows.

Inc row: K1, m1, k to last st, m1, k1
(28 sts).

Beg with a p row, stocking-st 7 rows

Shape big toe
Cast off 4 sts at beg of next 2 rows (20 sts).

Stocking-st 4 rows.

Dec row: (K2tog) to end (10 sts).

P 1 row.

Dec row: (K2tog) to end (5 sts).

Thread yarn through rem sts, pull tight and secure.

Hands and arms (make 2)
Beg at shoulder using the thumb method and A, cast on 12 sts.

Beg with a p row, stocking-st 5 rows.

Inc row: K1, m1, k to last st, m1, k1.

Rep last 6 rows 3 times more (20 sts).

Beg with a p row, stocking-st 9 rows.

Inc row: K1, m1, k to last st, m1, k1.

Rep last 10 rows once (24 sts).

P 1 row.

Change to B for hand.

Stocking-st 2 rows.

Inc row: K1, m1, k to last st, m1, k1
(26 sts).
Beg with a p row, stocking-st 5 rows.
Shape thumb
Cast off 4 sts at beg of next 2 rows (18 sts).
Stocking-st 4 rows.
Dec row: (K1, k2tog) to end
(12 sts).
Dec row: (P2tog) to end (6 sts).
Thread yarn through rem sts, pull tight
and secure.

Tail

Using B, cast on 8 sts.
Work in stocking-st until tail measures
9½in (24cm).
Thread yarn through sts, pull tight
and secure.

Banana

Beg at lower edge using the thumb
method and C, cast on 6 sts.
First and next 2 foll alt rows: P.
Inc row: (K1, inc) to end (9 sts).
Inc row: (K2, inc) to end (12 sts).
Inc row: (K3, inc) to end (15 sts).
Beg with a p row, stocking-st 7 rows.
Change to D and stocking-st 6 rows.
Dec row: (K3, k2tog) to end (12 sts).
Next and next foll alt row: P.
Dec row: (K2, k2tog) to end (9 sts).
Dec row: (K1, k2tog) to end (6 sts).
Thread yarn through rem sts, pull tight
and secure.

Skins (make 3)

Using the thumb method and C, cast
on 8 sts.
Beg with a p row, stocking-st 3 rows.
Dec row: K2, (k2tog) twice, k2 (6 sts).
Next and next foll alt row: P.
Dec row: K1, (k2tog) twice, k1 (4 sts).
Dec row: K2tog, k2tog tbl (2 sts).
Thread yarn through rem sts, pull tight
and secure.

Skin linings (make 3)

Using the thumb method and D, cast
on 6 sts.
Beg with a p row, stocking-st 3 rows.
Dec row: K1, (k2tog) twice, k1 (4 sts).
P 1 row.
Dec row: K2tog, k2tog tbl (2 sts).
Thread yarn through rem sts, pull tight
and secure.

Making up

Body

Place the two halves of body together
matching all edges and join row-ends. Stuff
body leaving neck and lower edge open.

Base

Pin base to lower edge of body and sew
base to body all the way round, adding
more stuffing to base if needed.

Head

Gather round cast-on sts of head, pull tight
and secure. Join row-ends leaving a gap,
stuff and close gap. Pin head to body,
adding more stuffing to neck if needed,
and stitch head in place by taking a small
horizontal st from head and then a small
horizontal st from body and doing this
alternately all the way round.

Legs and feet

Join row ends of legs and stuff. Fold feet in
half and join row-ends and stuff. Over-sew
cast-on sts of feet and sew feet to legs with
both big toes pointing inwards. Sew legs
to body.

Hands and arms

Fold cast-off sts of hands in half and join
row-ends of hands and sew round thumb.
Stuff hands. Fold cast-on sts of arms in
half and over-sew. Join row-ends of arms,
starting at shoulder using mattress-stitch,
stuffing as you go. With thumbs pointing
forwards, sew top of arms to 4th row below
neck at either side.

Muzzle

Join row-ends of muzzle and with this seam
at centre of underneath, join cast-off sts.
Stuff, then pin and sew muzzle to lower half
of head at centre front.

Monkeying around: There is plenty of evidence to show that monkeys have a mischievous sense of humour.

Eye piece
Sew eye piece to head, sitting it on top of muzzle, using back-stitch around outside edge.

Ears
Join row-ends of ears and with seam at centre back. Sew ears to head halfway down.

Tail
Join row-ends of tail on right side using mattress-stitch. Sew tail to body.

Banana
Gather round cast-on sts of banana and join row-ends, leaving a gap in the middle. Stuff, pushing stuffing into both ends with tweezers or the tip of scissors. Close gap and sew a running st along seam and pull tight and secure to make bend in banana.

Banana skins and skin linings
With wrong sides together, place a skin and a lining together matching all the edges and slip-stitch row-ends together. Do this for 3 skins. Place skins in a row and join row-ends of cast-on sts to form a ring around the banana. Position skins halfway up banana and sew cast-on sts of skin linings and skins to banana all the way round.

Embroidering the features
To make eyes, tie a knot in two lengths of black yarn winding the yarn round 6 times to make each knot (see page 122). Check that the knots are the same size. Tie eyes to head, with 5 clear knitted sts in between and run ends into head. Embroider nose in black taking a straight st over 2 sts and for mouth, a curved line in back-stitch with a straight st at each end. To begin and fasten off invisibly for the embroidery, tie a knot in end of yarn and take a big st through work, coming up to start embroidery. Allow knot to disappear through knitting and be caught in stuffing. To fasten off, take a few sts back and forth through work, inserting the needle where yarn comes out.

Snakes grow their entire lives. As long as there is food to eat, they just keep getting bigger. Many snakes regularly eat prey that is up to 20 percent of their body size (that's like you or I trying to stuff a whole watermelon in our mouth!) but they've been known to eat prey that is a lot, lot larger... Depending on the size of the meal, a snake may not eat again for several weeks or months.

SNAKES

DID YOU KNOW? Snakes can't hear the snake-charmer's flute; they just feel vibrations and that's why they dance.

What you'll need

Measurement
Each snake measures 23½in (60cm)
from head to tail

Materials
Any DK yarn:
50g khaki green (A – main colour
for first snake)
50g mulberry (A – main colour
for second snake)
50g black (B)
50g mustard (C)
Oddment of red (D)

*Note: amounts are generous
but approximate*
A pair of 3.25mm (US3:UK10) needles
Acrylic toy stuffing
Plastic-headed marker pins
Tweezers for stuffing small parts (optional)

Tension
26 sts x 34 rows measure 4in (10cm) square
over stocking-st using 3.25mm needles
before stuffing

Abbreviations
See page 124

How to make a Snake

Head
Beg at neck using the thumb method and A, cast on 30 sts.
P 1 row.
Inc row: K2, (m1, k2) to end (44 sts).
Beg with a p row, stocking-st 21 rows.
Dec row: (K2, k2tog) to end (33 sts).
P 1 row.
Dec row: (K1, k2tog) to end (22 sts).
Beg with a p row, stocking-st 9 rows.
Dec row: K1, (k2tog) to last st, k1 (12 sts).
Cast off p-wise.

Body
Beg at neck using the thumb method and B, cast on 30 sts.
P 1 row.
Commence stripe patt
Join on A and C and work in stripe as follows, carrying yarn loosely up side of work.

Beg with a k row, stocking-st 4 rows, C.
Stocking-st 2 rows, B.
Stocking-st 6 rows, A.
Stocking-st 2 rows, B.
This sets the stripe patt and is repeated for 120 more rows, ending 2 rows into the 10th stripe in A.

Shape tail
Keeping stripe patt correct, work 45 rows, decreasing 1 st at each end of next and every foll 4th row to 6 sts.
P 1 row.
Thread yarn through sts, pull tight and secure.

Tongue (make 2 pieces)
Using the thumb method and D, cast on 18 sts.
Cast off loosely, p-wise.

Eyes (make 2)
Using the thumb method and C, cast on 6 sts.
P 1 row.
Inc row: (Inc) to end (12 sts).
Beg with a p row, stocking-st 3 rows.
Change to B.
Stocking-st 2 rows.
Thread yarn through sts, pull tight and secure.

Eyelids (make 2)
Using the thumb method and A, cast on 10 sts.
Beg with a p row, stocking-st 2 rows, ending on a k row.
Dec row: (P2tog) to end (5 sts).
Thread yarn through rem sts, pull tight and secure.

Snakes have always had a bad press. What a shame!
They're really shy, retiring creatures who like to keep their own counsel.

Making up

Tongue

Place tongue pieces on top of each other matching all edges. Join two-thirds along the edges. Fan out ends into a Y-shape and stitch in place.

Body and head

Sew head to body by joining both sets of cast-on sts. Join row-ends of head and with seam at centre underneath, join cast-off sts of mouth, inserting tongue into this seam. Stuff head. With right sides outside and beginning at tail, join row-ends of body using mattress-stitch, stuffing lightly as you go and pushing stuffing into tip of tail with tweezers or tip of scissors.

Eyes

Join row-ends of eyes and gather round cast-on sts, pull tight and secure. Press eyes flat, like a button, and sew to head, with seam under the eyelid.

Eyelids

Sew eyelids to head, overlapping the eyes. Sew cast-on sts of lids to eyes.

Hippos are adapted for life in the water, spending up to 16 hours a day swimming, walking or wallowing in rivers and lakes. This keeps them nice and cool under the hot African sun. At sunset they'll leave their watery home in search of juicy grass to graze on, and will happily eat for five hours!

HIPPO

What you'll need

Measurement
Hippo measures 8¾in (22cm) in height

Materials
Any DK yarn:
100g blue grey (A)
Oddment of black for features
Note: amounts are generous but approximate
A pair of 3.25mm (US3:UK10) needles
Acrylic toy stuffing
Plastic-headed marker pins

Tension
26 sts x 34 rows measure 4in (10cm) square over stocking-st using 3.25mm needles before stuffing

Abbreviations
See page 124

How to make Hippo

Body (make 2 pieces)

Beg at lower edge using the thumb method and A, cast on 35 sts.

First and next 4 foll alt rows: P.

Inc row: K10, m1, k15, m1, k10 (37 sts).
Inc row: K11, m1, k15, m1, k11 (39 sts).
Inc row: K12, m1, k15, m1, k12 (41 sts).
Inc row: K13, m1, k15, m1, k13 (43 sts).
Inc row: K14, m1, k15, m1, k14 (45 sts).
Beg with a p row, stocking-st 11 rows.
Dec row: K2tog, k to last 2 sts, k2tog tbl.
Next row: P.
Rep last 2 rows 12 more times (19 sts).
Cast off.

Base

Using the thumb method and A, cast on 20 sts.

First row: P.

Inc row: K1, m1, k to last st, m1, k1.
Rep first 2 rows 5 more times (32 sts).
Beg with a p row, stocking-st 5 rows.
Dec row: K2tog, k to last 2 sts, k2tog tbl.
Next row: P.
Rep last 2 rows 5 more times (20 sts).
Cast off.

Head

Using the thumb method and A, cast on 22 sts.
Place a marker at centre of cast-on sts.
P 1 row.

Inc row: K2, (m1, k2) to end (32 sts).
Beg with a p row, stocking-st 3 rows.
Inc row: K2, (m1, k4) to last 2 sts, m1, k2 (40 sts).
Beg with a p row, stocking-st 3 rows.
Inc row: K6, (m1, k1) 10 times, k8, (k1, m1) 10 times, k6 (60 sts).
Beg with a p row, stocking-st 21 rows.

Shape top of head

Dec row: (K4, k2tog) to end (50 sts).
Next and next 3 foll alt rows: P.
Dec row: (K3, k2tog) to end (40 sts).
Dec row: (K2, k2tog) to end (30 sts).
Dec row: (K1, k2tog) to end (20 sts).
Dec row: (K2tog) to end (10 sts).
Thread yarn through rem sts, pull tight and secure.

Snout

Beg at centre using the thumb method and A, cast on 24 sts.
Place a marker at centre of cast-on sts.
P 1 row.
Inc row: K4, (m1, k1) 6 times, k4, (k1, m1) 6 times, k4 (36 sts).

Beg with a p row, stocking-st 3 rows.
Inc row: K4, (m1, k2) 6 times, k4, (k2, m1) 6 times, k4 (48 sts).
Beg with a p row, stocking-st 11 rows.
Dec row: (K4, k2tog) to end (40 sts).
P 1 row.
Cast off.

Hind legs (make 2)

Note: follow individual instructions for right and left legs.
Beg at sole using the thumb method and A, cast on 22 sts.
Place a marker at centre of cast-on sts.
P 1 row.
Inc row: K1, (m1, k1) to end (43 sts).
Beg with a p row, stocking-st 17 rows.
Dec for right leg: K4, (k2tog) 10 times, k19 (33 sts).
Dec for left leg: K19, (k2tog) 10 times, k4 (33 sts).
Beg with a p row, stocking-st 5 rows.
Cast off 9 sts at beg of next 2 rows (15 sts).
Dec row: (K2tog) twice, k to last 4 sts, k2tog, k2tog tbl.
Dec row: P2tog tbl, p to last 2 sts, p2tog.
Rep last 2 rows once (3 sts).
Cast off.

Forelegs (make 2)

Beg at lower edge using the thumb method and A, cast on 14 sts.
First and next 3 foll alt rows: P.
Inc row: K2, (m1, k2) to end (20 sts).
Inc row: (K1, m1, k8, m1, k1) twice (24 sts).
Inc row: (K1, m1, k10, m1, k1) twice (28 sts).
Inc row: (K1, m1, k12, m1, k1) twice (32 sts).
Beg with a p row, stocking-st 3 rows.
Dec row: (K1, k2tog, k10, k2tog tbl, k1) twice (28 sts).

DID YOU KNOW? A hippopotamus has no sweat glands. They roll around in mud or dunk into water to keep cool.

Next and next foll alt row: P.
Dec row: (K1, k2tog, k8, k2tog tbl, k1)
twice (24 sts).
Dec row: (K1, k2tog, k6, k2tog tbl, k1)
twice (20 sts).
Beg with a p row, stocking-st 11 rows.
Dec row: (K2tog) to end (10 sts).
Cast off p-wise.

Ears (make 2)
Beg at lower edge using the thumb method
and A, cast on 8 sts.
P 1 row.
Inc row: K1, (m1, k1) to end (15 sts).
Beg with a p row, stocking-st 5 rows.
Dec row: (K1, k2tog) to end (10 sts).
Thread yarn through rem sts, pull tight
and secure.

Tail
Using the thumb method and A, cast on
8 sts.
Beg with a p row, stocking-st 9 rows.
Cast off.

Making up
Body
Place the two halves of body together
matching all edges and join row-ends. Stuff
body leaving neck and lower edge open.

Base
Pin base to lower edge of body and sew
base to body all the way round, adding
more stuffing to base if needed.

Head
Join row-ends of head and stuff. Bring
marker at cast-on edge and seam together
and over-sew cast-on sts. Place cast-on sts
of head at centre front of neck with seam
underneath and join, adding more stuffing
to neck if needed. Sew back of head to
neck by taking a small horizontal st from
head then a small horizontal st from neck
and doing this alternately all the way round.

Snout
Join row-ends of snout. Bringing row-ends
and marker together join cast-on sts. Stuff
snout and with seam at centre, underneath,
pin and sew snout to centre of lower half
of head.

Hind legs
Join row-ends of hind legs and bringing
marker and seam together, over-sew cast-on
sts. Stuff legs, pushing stuffing into toes.
Stand body on flat surface and pin legs to
body. Sew legs to body all the way round.

Forelegs
Fold cast-on sts of forelegs in half and over-
sew. Fold cast-off sts in half and over-sew.
Join row-ends leaving a gap, stuff and close
gap. Sew forelegs to either side of body,
sewing cast-off sts to neck.

Ears
Join row-ends of ears and with seam at
centre back, sew ears to head.

Tail
Make a small tassel in A (see page 122)
and anchor it to inside edge of one end
of tail. Gather round this end and pull tight
and secure. Join row-ends of tail on right
side using mattress-stitch. Sew tail to back
of hippo.

Embroidering the features
To make eyes, tie a knot in two lengths of
black yarn winding the yarn round 6 times
to make each knot (see page 122). Check
that the knots are the same size. Tie eyes
to head on 2nd row above snout with 8
clear knitted sts in between and run ends
into head. Embroider nostrils in black taking
2 straight sts close together for each nostril
at sides of snout. For mouth, embroider
a curved line in back-stitch with a straight
st at each end. To begin and fasten off
invisibly for embroidery, tie a knot in end
of yarn and take a big st through work,
coming up to start embroidery. Allow the
knot to disappear through knitting and be
caught in stuffing. To fasten off, take a few
sts back and forth through work, inserting
the needle where yarn comes out.

A group of rhinos is called a 'crash' – an appropriate term for a large animal that can crash through just about anything in its way. Rhinos may look indestructible, but their skin is actually quite sensitive, especially to sunburn and biting insects. That's why they like to wallow in mud.

RHINO

What you'll need

Measurement

Rhino measures 8¾in (22cm)
in height

Materials

Any DK yarn:
100g grey (A)
20g white (B)
Oddment of black for features
*Note: amounts are generous
but approximate*
A pair of 3.25mm (US3:UK10)
needles
Acrylic toy stuffing
Plastic-headed marker pins
Tweezers for stuffing small parts
(optional)

Tension

26 sts x 34 rows measure 4in (10cm)
square over stocking-st using 3.25mm
needles before stuffing

Abbreviations

See page 124

DID YOU KNOW? Rhino horns can grow again. They're made of compressed keratin fibres, just like our fingernails.

rhino

How to make Rhino

Body (make 2 pieces)

Beg at lower edge using the thumb method and A, cast on 35 sts.

First and next 4 foll alt rows: P.

Inc row: K10, m1, k15, m1, k10 (37 sts).

Inc row: K11, m1, k15, m1, k11 (39 sts).

Inc row: K12, m1, k15, m1, k12 (41 sts).

Inc row: K13, m1, k15, m1, k13 (43 sts).

Inc row: K14, m1, k15, m1, k14 (45 sts).

Beg with a p row, stocking-st 11 rows.

Dec row: K2tog, k to last 2 sts, k2tog tbl.

Next row: P.

Rep last 2 rows 12 more times (19 sts). Cast off.

Base

Using the thumb method and A, cast on 20 sts.

First row: P.

Inc row: K1, m1, k to last st, m1, k1.

Rep first 2 rows 5 more times (32 sts).

Beg with a p row, stocking-st 5 rows.

Dec row: K2tog, k to last 2 sts, k2tog tbl.

Next row: P.

Rep last 2 rows 5 more times (20 sts). Cast off.

Head

Beg at lower front edge using the thumb method and A, cast on 22 sts.

Place a marker at centre of cast-on sts.

P 1 row.

Inc row: K2, (m1, k2) to end (32 sts).

Beg with a p row, stocking-st 3 rows.

Inc row: K2, (m1, k4) to last 2 sts, m1, k1 (40 sts).

Beg with a p row, stocking-st 3 rows.

Inc row: K8, (m1, k1) 5 times, k14, (k1, m1) 5 times, k8 (50 sts).

Beg with a p row, stocking-st 21 rows.

Shape top of head

Dec row: (K3, k2tog) to end (40 sts).

Next and next 2 foll alt rows: P.

Dec row: (K2, k2tog) to end (30 sts).

Dec row: (K1, k2tog) to end (20 sts).

Dec row: (K2tog) to end (10 sts).

Thread yarn through rem sts, pull tight and secure.

Snout

Using the thumb method and A, cast on 40 sts.

Beg with a p row, stocking-st 3 rows.

Dec row: (K8, k2tog twice, k8) twice (36 sts).

Beg with a p row, stocking-st 3 rows.

Dec row: (K7, k2tog twice, k7) twice (32 sts).

Beg with a p row, stocking-st 3 rows.

Dec row: (K6, k2tog twice, k6) twice (28 sts).

Beg with a p row, stocking-st 9 rows.

Garter-st 2 rows.

Dec row: (K2, k2tog twice, k2, k2tog twice, k2) twice (20 sts).

P 1 row.

Dec row: (K3, k2tog twice, k3) twice (16 sts).

Dec row: (P2, p2tog twice, p2) twice (12 sts).

Cast off.

Hind legs (make 2)

Using the thumb method and A, cast on 36 sts.

Beg with a p row, stocking-st 21 rows.

P 2 rows.

Dec row: (K2, k2tog) to end (27 sts).

Next and next foll alt row: P.

Dec row: (K1, k2tog) to end (18 sts).

Dec row: (K2tog) to end (9 sts).

Thread yarn through rem sts, pull tight and secure.

Forelegs (make 2)

Beg at shoulder using the thumb method and A, cast on 14 sts.

P 1 row.

Inc row: K1, (m1, k1) (27 sts).

Beg with a p row, stocking-st 25 rows.

P 2 rows.

Dec row: (K1, k2tog) to end (18 sts).

Yes, the horse has been around as long as I have, but I've got horns. Two, actually.

P 1 row.
Dec row: (K2tog) to end (9 sts).
Thread yarn through rem sts, pull tight and secure.

Large horn

Beg at base using the thumb method and B, cast on 16 sts.
Beg with a p row, stocking-st 5 rows.
Dec row: K5, k2tog, k2, k2tog, k5 (14 sts).
Next and next 3 foll alt rows: P.
Dec row: K4, k2tog, k2, k2tog, k4 (12 sts).
Dec row: K3, k2tog, k2, k2tog, k3 (10 sts).
Dec row: K2, k2tog, k2, k2tog, k2 (8 sts).
Dec row: (K2tog) to end (4 sts).
Thread yarn through rem sts, pull tight and secure.

Small horn

Beg at base using the thumb method and B, cast on 12 sts.
Beg with a p row, stocking-st 3 rows.
Dec row: K3, k2tog, k2, k2tog, k3 (10 sts).
Next and next foll alt row: P.
Dec row: K2, k2tog, k2, k2tog, k2 (8 sts).
Dec row: (K2tog) to end (4 sts).
Thread yarn through rem sts, pull tight and secure.

Ears (make 2)

Beg at base using the thumb method and A, cast on 14 sts.
P 1 row.
Inc row: K2, (m1, k2) to end (20 sts).
Beg with a p row, stocking-st 3 rows.
Dec row: K2tog twice, k12, k2tog, k2tog tbl (16 sts).
Beg with a p row, stocking-st 3 rows.
Dec row: K2tog twice, k8, k2tog, k2tog tbl (12 sts).
P 1 row.
Dec row: (K2tog) to end (6 sts).
Thread yarn through rem sts, pull tight and secure.

Tail

Using the thumb method and A, cast on 8 sts.
Beg with a p row, stocking-st 9 rows.
Cast off.

Making up

Body

Place two halves of the body together matching all edges and join row-ends. Stuff body leaving neck and lower edge open.

Base

Pin base to lower edge of body and sew base to body all the way round, adding more stuffing to base if needed.

Head

Join row-ends of head and stuff. Bring the marker at cast-on edge and seam together and over-sew cast-on sts. Place cast-on sts of head at centre front of neck with seam underneath and join, adding more stuffing to neck if needed. Sew back of head to neck by taking a small horizontal st from head then a small horizontal st from neck and doing this alternately all the way round.

Snout

Join row-ends of snout and with seam at centre of underneath, over-sew cast-off sts. Stuff snout and with seam at centre of underneath, pin and sew snout to centre of lower half of head.

Hind legs

Join row-ends of hind legs and stuff, leaving cast-on sts at top of legs open. Stand body on flat surface and pin legs to body. Sew legs to body all the way round.

Forelegs

Join row-ends of forelegs and stuff. With seam at centre of inside edge, over-sew cast-on sts and sew forelegs to either side of body, sewing cast-on sts to neck.

Ears

Join row-ends of ears with seam at centre back and fold cast-on sts of ears in half and over-sew. Sew ears to head.

Horns

Join row-ends of each horn and stuff, pushing stuffing into tips with tweezers. Sew horns to snout with seams at centre back, the small horn behind the large horn.

Tail

Make a small tassel in A (see page 122) and anchor it to inside edge of one end of tail. Gather round this end, pull tight and secure. Join row-ends of tail on right side using mattress-stitch. Sew tail to back of rhino.

Embroidering the features

To make eyes, tie a knot in two lengths of black yarn winding the yarn round 6 times to make each knot (see page 122). Check that the knots are the same size. Tie eyes to head on 4th row above snout with 7 clear knitted sts in between and run ends into head.

rhino

Warthogs can weigh as much as 330lbs (150kg). They may not be the most beautiful or graceful of creatures, but they have remarkable strength, flexibility and intelligence! Instead of wasting time digging their own burrows they find abandoned ones which they enter back-end first ready to burst out at any moment.

WARTHOG

Warthogs love to jump up and down on the spot!

What you'll need

Measurement
Warthog measures 8½in (22cm) in height

Materials
100g rust (A)
20g white (B)
Oddment of black for features
*Note: amounts are generous
but approximate*
A pair of 3.25mm (US3:UK10) needles
Acrylic toy stuffing
Plastic-headed marker pins
Tweezers for stuffing small parts (optional)

Tension
26 sts x 34 rows measure 4in (10cm) square
over stocking-st using 3.25mm (US3:UK10)
needles before stuffing

Abbreviations
See page 124

How to make Warthog

Body (make 2 pieces)
Beg at lower edge using the thumb method and A, cast on 35 sts.
First and next 4 foll alt rows: P.
Inc row: K10, m1, k15, m1, k10 (37 sts).
Inc row: K11, m1, k15, m1, k11 (39 sts).
Inc row: K12, m1, k15, m1, k12 (41 sts).
Inc row: K13, m1, k15, m1, k13 (43 sts).
Inc row: K14, m1, k15, m1, k14 (45 sts).
Beg with a p row, stocking-st 11 rows.
Dec row: K2tog, k to last 2 sts, k2tog tbl.
Next row: P.
Rep last 2 rows 12 more times (19 sts).
Cast off.

Base
Using the thumb method and A, cast on 20 sts.
First row: P.
Inc row: K1, m1, k to last st, m1, k1.
Rep first 2 rows 5 more times (32 sts).
Beg with a p row, stocking-st 5 rows.
Dec row: K2tog, k to last 2 sts, k2tog tbl.
Next row: P.
Rep last 2 rows 5 more times (20 sts).
Cast off.

Head
Beg at lower front edge using the thumb method and A, cast on 22 sts.
Place a marker at centre of cast-on sts.
P 1 row.
Inc row: K2, (m1, k2) to end (32 sts).
Beg with a p row, stocking-st 3 rows.
Inc row: K2, (m1, k4) to last 2 sts, m1, k2 (40 sts).
Beg with a p row, stocking-st 3 rows.
Inc row: K8, (m1, k1) 5 times, k14, (k1, m1) 5 times, k8 (50 sts).
Beg with a p row, stocking-st 21 rows.

Shape top of head
Dec row: (K3, k2tog) to end (40 sts).
Next and 2 foll alt rows: P.
Dec row: (K2, k2tog) to end (30 sts).
Dec row: (K1, k2tog) to end (20 sts).
Dec row: (K2tog) to end (10 sts).
Thread yarn through rem sts, pull tight and secure.

Snout
Using the thumb method and A, cast on 40 sts.
Beg with a p row, stocking-st 3 rows.
Dec row: (K8, k2tog twice, k8) twice (36 sts).
Beg with a p row, stocking-st 3 rows.
Dec row: (K7, k2tog twice, k7) twice (32 sts).
Beg with a p row, stocking-st 3 rows.
Dec row: (K6, k2tog twice, k6) twice (28 sts).
Beg with a p row, stocking-st 3 rows.
Work ridge to mark edge of snout.

Beg with a p row, stocking-st 2 rows ending on a k row.
Dec row: (K2, k2tog twice, k2, k2tog twice, k2) twice (20 sts).
Next and next foll alt row: P.
Dec row: (K3, k2tog twice, k3) twice (16 sts).
Dec row: (K2, k2tog twice, k2) twice (12 sts).
Cast off, p-wise.

Hind legs (make 2)
Beg at hoof using the thumb method and A, cast on 13 sts.
P 1 row.
Inc row: K1, (m1, k1) to end (25 sts).
Beg with a p row, stocking-st 5 rows.
Garter-st 2 rows.
Beg with a k row, stocking-st 4 rows.
Dec row: K1, (k2tog, k1) to end (17 sts).
Beg with a p row, stocking-st 3 rows.
Inc row: (K2, m1) twice, k9, (m1, k2) twice (21 sts).
Next and next 6 foll alt rows: P.
Inc row: K3, m1, k15, m1, k3 (23 sts).
Inc row: K4, m1, k15, m1, k4 (25 sts).
Inc row: K5, m1, k15, m1, k5 (27 sts).
Inc row: K6, m1, k15, m1, k6 (29 sts).
Inc row: K7, m1, k15, m1, k7 (31 sts).
Inc row: K8, m1, k15, m1, k8 (33 sts).
Inc row: K9, m1, k15, m1, k9 (35 sts).
P 1 row.
Cast off.

Forelegs (make 2)
Beg at hoof using the thumb method and A, cast on 8 sts.
P 1 row.
Inc row: K1, (m1, k1) to end (15 sts).
Beg with a p row, stocking-st 5 rows.
Garter-st 2 rows.
Beg with a k row, stocking-st 4 rows.
Dec row: (K1, k2tog) to end (10 sts).
Beg with a p row, stocking-st 3 rows.

Inc row: K2, (m1, k2) to end (14 sts).
Next and next 4 foll alt rows: P.
Inc row: K2, m1, k10, m1, k2 (16 sts).
Inc row: K3, m1, k10, m1, k3 (18 sts).
Inc row: K4, m1, k10, m1, k4 (20 sts).
Inc row: K5, m1, k10, m1, k5 (22 sts).
Inc row: K6, m1, k10, m1, k6 (24 sts).
Beg with a p row, stocking-st 5 rows.
Dec row: (K4, k2tog twice, k4) twice
(20 sts).
Next and next foll alt row: P.
Dec row: (k3, k2tog twice, k3) twice
(16 sts).
Dec row: (k2, k2tog twice, k2) twice
(12 sts).
P 1 row.
Cast off.

Tusks (make 2)
Beg at lower edge using the thumb method
and B, cast on 8 sts.
Beg with a p row, stocking-st 7 rows.
Dec row: K1, k2tog, k2, k2tog k1 (6 sts).
Beg with a p row, stocking-st 3 rows.
Dec row: K1, (k2tog) twice, k1 (4 sts).
Thread yarn through rem sts, pull tight
and secure.

Ears (make 4 pieces)
Cast on 10 sts.
Beg with a p row, stocking-st 3 rows.
Dec row: K2, k2tog, k2, k2tog, k2 (8 sts).
Beg with a p row, stocking-st 3 rows.
Dec row: K1, k2tog, k2, k2tog, k1 (6 sts).
Beg with a p row, stocking-st 3 rows.
Dec row: (k2tog) to end (3 sts).
Thread yarn through rem sts, pull tight
and secure.

Warts (make 4)
Note: 2 separate balls of A are required.
Using the thumb method and one strand
of A, cast on 12 sts.

Join on second ball of A and treat
the 2 strands as one.
P 1 row.
Dec row: (K2tog) to end (6 sts).
Thread yarn through rem sts, pull tight
and secure.

Tail
Using A, cast on 6 sts.
Work in stocking-st for 3in (8cm).
Cast off.

Making up
Body
Place the two halves of body together
matching all edges and join row-ends. Stuff
body leaving neck and lower edge open.

Base
Pin base to lower edge of body and sew
base to body all the way round, adding
more stuffing to base if needed.

Head
Join row-ends of head and stuff. Bring
marker at cast-on edge and seam together
and over-sew cast-on sts. Place cast-on sts
of head at centre front of neck with seam
underneath and join, adding more stuffing
to neck if needed. Sew back of head to
neck by taking a small horizontal st from
head then a small horizontal st from neck
and doing this alternately all the way round.

Snout
Join row-ends of snout and with seam at
centre at underneath, over-sew cast-off
sts. Stuff snout and with seam at centre of
underneath, pin and sew snout to centre
of lower half of head.

Warthog: Seen here reversing into his new home.

Warthog: Seen resting after a day filled with rain and pogoing.

Hind legs

Join row-ends of hooves and with seam at centre, underneath, join cast-on sts. Join row-ends of ankle and stuff hoof and ankle. Join row-ends of leg and stuff. To shape hoof, take a length of black yarn and sew a large st around centre of hoof, starting and finishing at centre back of garter-sts of hoof. Pull tight and knot yarn sewing ends into hoof. Place body on a flat surface and pin legs to body and sew cast-off sts of legs to body all the way round.

Forelegs

Make up as for hind legs with seam at centre of inside edge. Shape hooves as for hind legs. Sew forelegs to body at each side, sewing cast-off sts to neck.

Tusks

Join row-ends of tusks and stuff, pushing stuffing in with tweezers or tip of scissors. Gather round cast-on sts, pull tight and secure. Sew tusks to either side of snout, as in picture.

Ears

Place the two pieces of ears together matching all edges and join row-ends. Sew ears to head.

Warts

Join row-ends of cast-on sts of warts. Sew outer edge of 2 warts to each side of snout and 2 warts to head.

Tail

Make a small tassel (see page 122) using black yarn and anchor it to inside edge of one end of the tail. Gather round this end and pull tight and secure. Join row-ends of tail on right side using mattress-stitch. Sew tail to back of warthog.

Embroidering the features

To make eyes, tie a knot in two lengths of black yarn winding the yarn round 6 times to make each knot (see page 122). Check that the knots are the same size. Tie eyes on head to 4th row above snout with 6 clear knitted sts in between and run ends into head.

Koalas live almost entirely on eucalyptus leaves, grinding them with special cheek teeth. These tough leaves are poisonous to most other animals. Koala bears don't usually drink water as they get enough moisture from the leaves. However, this diet doesn't provide many calories, so koalas conserve energy by resting for as much as 20 hours each day.

KOALA

What you'll need

Measurement
Koala measures 9½in (24cm) in height

Materials
Any DK yarn:
50g white (A)
100g grey (B)
20g black (C)
Note: amounts are generous but approximate
A pair of 3.25mm (US3:UK10) needles
Acrylic toy stuffing
Plastic-headed marker pins

Tension
26 sts x 34 rows measure 4in
(10cm) square over stocking-st using
3.25mm needles before stuffing

Abbreviations
See page 124

DID YOU KNOW? A newborn koala is only the size of a jelly bean.

How to make Koala

Body (make 1 piece in A and 1 piece in B)

Beg at lower edge using the thumb method and A or B, cast on 29 sts.

First and next 4 foll alt rows: P.

Inc row: K7, m1, k15, m1, k7 (31 sts).

Inc row: K8, m1, k15, m1, k8 (33 sts).

Inc row: K9, m1, k15, m1, k9 (35 sts).

Beg with a p row, stocking-st 29 rows.

Dec row: K2tog, k to last 2 sts, k2tog tbl.

Next row: P.

Rep last 2 rows 5 more times (23 sts).

Cast off.

Base

Using the thumb method and A, cast on 16 sts.

First row: P.

Inc row: K1, m1, k to last st, m1, k1.

Rep first 2 rows 4 more times (26 sts).

Beg with a p row, stocking-st 5 rows.

Dec row: K2tog, k to last 2 sts, k2tog tbl.

Next row: P.

Rep last 2 rows 4 more times (16 sts).

Cast off.

Head

Beg at lower edge using the thumb method and B, cast on 8 sts.

First and next 6 foll alt rows: P.

Inc row: (Inc) to end (16 sts).

Inc row: (K1, inc) to end (24 sts).

Inc row: (K2, inc) to end (32 sts).

Inc row: (K3, inc) to end (40 sts).

Inc row: (K4, inc) to end (48 sts).

Inc row: (K5, inc) to end (56 sts).

Inc row: (K6, inc) to end (64 sts).

Beg with a p row, stocking-st 3 rows.

Inc row: K29, (m1, k2) 4 times, k27 (68 sts).

Next and next 2 foll alt rows: P.

Inc row: K31, (m1, k2) 4 times, k29 (72 sts).

Inc row: K33, (m1, k2) 4 times, k31 (76 sts).

Inc row: K35, (m1, k2) 4 times, k33 (80 sts).

Beg with a p row stocking-st 7 rows.

Dec row: K33, (k2tog, k2) 4 times, k31 (76 sts).

Beg with a p row, stocking-st 3 rows.

Dec row: K31, (k2tog, k2) 4 times, k29 (72 sts).

Beg with a p row, stocking-st 3 rows.

Shape top of head

Dec row: (K7, k2tog) to end (64 sts).

Next and next 6 foll alt rows: P.

Dec row: (K6, k2tog) to end (56 sts).

Dec row: (K5, k2tog) to end (48 sts).

Dec row: (K4, k2tog) to end (40 sts).

Dec row: (K3, k2tog) to end (32 sts).

Dec row: (K2, k2tog) to end (24 sts).

Dec row: (K1, k2tog) to end (16 sts).

Dec row: (K2tog) to end (8 sts).

Thread yarn through rem sts, pull tight and secure.

Hind legs (make 2)

Beg at toes using the thumb method and B, cast on 24 sts.

First and next foll alt row: P.

Inc row: (K5, m1, k2, m1, k5) twice (28 sts).

Inc row: (K6, m1, k2, m1, k6) twice (32 sts).

Beg with a p row, stocking-st 5 rows.

Inc row: (K7, m1, k2, m1, k7) twice (36 sts).

Beg with a p row, stocking-st 5 rows.

Shape leg

Row 1: K27, turn.

Row 2: S1p, p17, turn.

Row 3: S1k, k to end.

Rows 4–6: Beg with a p row, stocking-st 3 rows.

Rep last 6 rows 3 more times.

Dec row: K5, (k2tog) 4 times, k10, (k2tog) 4 times, k5 (28 sts).

P 1 row.

Cast off.

Arms (make 2)

Beg at paw using the thumb method and B, cast on 16 sts.

First and next foll alt row: P.

Inc row: (K3, m1, k2, m1, k3) twice (20 sts).

Inc row: (K4, m1, k2, m1, k4) twice (24 sts).

Beg with a p row, stocking-st 5 rows.

Inc row: (K5, m1, k2, m1, k5) twice (28 sts).

Beg with a p row, stocking-st 5 rows.

Inc row: (K6, m1, k2, m1, k6) twice (32 sts).

Beg with a p row, stocking-st 5 rows.

Shape arm

Row 1: K24, turn.

Row 2: S1p, p15, turn.

Row 3: S1k, k to end.

Row 4: P.

Rows 5–8: Beg with a k row, stocking-st 4 rows.

Rep last 8 rows once more.

Dec row: K4, (k2tog) 4 times, k8, (k2tog) 4 times, k4 (24 sts).

P 1 row.

Cast off.

Nose

Note: nose is knitted in garter-st.

Beg at lower edge using the thumb method and C, cast on 4 sts.

Inc row: Inc, k2, inc (6 sts).

K 1 row.

Inc row: Inc, k4, inc (8 sts).

Garter-st 15 rows.

Dec row: K2tog, k4, k2tog tbl (6 sts).
K 1 row.
Dec row: K2tog, k2, k2tog tbl (4 sts).
Cast off k-wise.

Ears (make 2 outside ear pieces and 2 inside ear pieces)

Special abbreviation: loop-st
Insert RH needle into next st, place first finger of LH behind LH needle and wind yarn round needle and finger twice, then just round needle once. Knit st, pulling 3 loops through. Place these loops on LH needle and knit into the back of them. Pull loops sharply down to secure. Cont to next st.

Outside ear piece

Beg at lower edge using the thumb method and B, cast on 4 sts.
First and next 4 foll alt rows: P.
Inc row: (Inc) to end (8 sts).
Inc row: (K1, inc) to end (12 sts).
Inc row: (K2, inc) to end (16 sts).
Inc row: (K3, inc) to end (20 sts).
Inc row: (K4, inc) to end (24 sts).
P 1 row.
Cast off loosely.

Inside ear piece

Note: follow instructions for 1 right and 1 left inside ear piece.
Beg at lower edge using the thumb method and B, cast on 4 sts.
First and next 4 foll alt rows: P.
Inc row: (Inc) to end (8 sts).
Inc row: (K1, inc) to end (12 sts).
Inc row: (K2, inc) to end (16 sts).
Inc row: (K3, inc) to end (20 sts).
Inc row: (K4, inc) to end (24 sts).

Right ear

Break off B and change to A.
Next row: (WS facing) p1, yb, (loop-st) 14 times, p1, turn.
Cast off 16 sts k-wise (8 sts).
Re-join B.

P 1 row.
Cast off.
Left ear
Next row: (WS facing) p8, join on A and continue across row and p1, yb, (loop-st) 14 times, p1.
Cast off 16 sts k-wise (8 sts).
Using B, cast off rem sts.

Making up
Body
Place two halves of body together matching all edges and join row-ends. Stuff body leaving neck and lower edge open.

Base
Pin base to lower edge of body and sew base to body all the way round, adding more stuffing to base if needed.

Head
Gather round cast-on sts of head, pull tight and secure. Join row-ends of head leaving gap. Stuff, pushing a ball of stuffing into nose, and close gap. Pin head to body adding more stuffing to neck if needed. Sew head in place by taking a small horizontal st from head and then a small horizontal st from body and doing this alternately all the way round.

Hind legs
Join row-ends of each hind leg and with seam at centre of inside edge, join cast-on sts. Stuff and join cast-off sts. Place koala on a flat surface and pin legs to body. Curl legs round body and sew in place.

Arms
Join row-ends of each arm and with seam at centre of inside edge, join cast-on sts. Stuff and join cast-off sts. Attach arms to koala sewing shoulders to neck and with paws sloping down.

Nose
Sew outside edge of nose to head.

Embroidering the features
To make eyes, tie a knot in 2 lengths of black yarn winding the yarn round 6 times to make each knot (see page 122). Check that the knots are the same size. Tie eyes to 4th row above top of nose with 7 clear knitted sts in between. Run ends into head. Work a chain-stitch in black round outside edge of nose. On all paws, embroider 3 toes in black taking three straight sts at ends of paws, beginning and fastening off invisibly. To begin and fasten off for the embroidery, tie a knot in end of yarn and take a big st through work, coming up to start embroidery. Allow knot to disappear through knitting and be caught in stuffing. To fasten off, take a few sts back and forth through work, inserting the needle where yarn comes out.

Ears
With wrong sides facing, place a piece of outside ear and inside ear together, matching all edges. Tuck inside the cast-off sts of outside edge and join outside edges. Join row-ends of lower edge and sew both ears to head of koala. Finally, cut loops of ears.

The moose is the largest deer in the world, native to North America, Europe and Asia, where they live in mountain meadows and forests. The largest moose weighed in at 1,800lb (820kg) and was 7½ft (2.3m) tall. Moose have compact bodies with long, powerful legs, so they are excellent runners.

MOOSE

No, our moose isn't crying. He's showing us that he has very poor eyesight.

What you'll need

Measurement

Moose measures 8¾in (22cm) in height, excluding antlers

Materials

Any DK yarn:
100g brown (A)
25g beige (B)
25g cream (C)
Oddment of black for features
Note: amounts are generous but approximate
A pair of 3.25mm (US3:UK10) needles
Acrylic toy stuffing
Plastic-headed marker pins

Tension

26 sts x 34 rows measure 4in (10cm) square over stocking-st using 3.25mm needles before stuffing

Abbreviations

See page 124

moose

How to make Moose

Body (make 2 pieces)
Beg at lower edge using the thumb method and A, cast on 35 sts.
First and next 4 foll alt rows: P.
Inc row: K10, m1, k15, m1, k10 (37 sts).
Inc row: K11, m1, k15, m1, k11 (39 sts).
Inc row: K12, m1, k15, m1, k12 (41 sts).
Inc row: K13, m1, k15, m1, k13 (43 sts).
Inc row: K14, m1, k15, m1, k14 (45 sts).
Beg with a p row, stocking-st 11 rows.
Dec row: K2tog, k to last 2 sts, k2tog tbl.
Next row: P.
Rep last 2 rows 12 times more (19 sts).
Cast off.

Base
Using the thumb method and A, cast on 20 sts.
First row: P.
Inc row: K1, m1, k to last st, m1, k1.
Rep these 2 rows 5 times more (32 sts).
Beg with a p row, work 5 rows stocking-st.
Dec row: K2tog, k to last 2 sts, k2tog tbl.
Next row: P.
Rep last 2 rows 5 times more (20 sts).
Cast off.

Head
Beg at lower front edge using the thumb method and A, cast on 22 sts.
Place a marker at centre of cast-on sts.
P1 row.
Inc row: K2, (m1, k2) to end (32 sts).
Beg with a p row, stocking-st 3 rows.
Inc row: K2, (m1, k4) to last 2 sts, m1, k2 (40 sts).
Beg with a p row, stocking-st 3 rows.
Inc row: K8, (m1, k1) 5 times, k14, (k1, m1) 5 times, k8 (50 sts).
Beg with a p row, stocking-st 21 rows.

Shape top of head
Dec row: (K3, k2tog) to end (40 sts).
Next and next 2 foll alt rows: P.
Dec row: (K2, k2tog) to end (30 sts).
Dec row: (K1, k2tog) to end (20 sts).
Dec row: (K2tog) to end (10 sts).
Thread yarn through rem sts, pull tight and secure.

Snout
Beg at lower edge using the thumb method and A, cast on 18 sts.
Place a marker at centre of cast-on sts.
P 1 row.
Inc row: K4, (m1, k1) 3 times, k4, (k1, m1) 3 times, k4 (24 sts).
Beg with a p row, stocking-st 3 rows.
Inc row: K4, (m1, k1) 6 times, k4, (k1, m1) 6 times, k4 (36 sts).
Beg with a p row, stocking-st 9 rows.
Dec row: (K4, k2tog) to end (30 sts).
Beg with a p row, stocking-st 7 rows.
Cast off.

Hind legs (make 2)
Beg at hoof using the thumb method and B cast on 13 sts.
P 1 row.
Inc row: K1, (m1, k1) to end (25 sts).
Beg with a p row, stocking-st 5 rows.
Garter-st 2 rows.
Change to A.
Beg with a k row, stocking-st 4 rows.
Dec row: K1, (k2tog, k1) to end (17 sts).
Beg with a p row, stocking-st 3 rows.
Inc row: K1, (m1, k3) to last st, m1, k1.
P 1 row.
Rep last inc row once (31 sts).
Beg with a p row, stocking-st 13 rows.
Dec row: K1, (k2tog, k1) to end (21 sts).
P 1 row.
Cast off.

Forelegs (make 2)
Beg at hoof using the thumb method and A, cast on 8 sts.
P 1 row.
Inc row: K1, (m1, k1) to end (15 sts).
Beg with a p row, stocking-st 5 rows.
Garter-st 2 rows.
Change to A.
Beg with a k row, stocking-st 4 rows.
Dec row: (K1, k2tog) to end (10 sts).
Beg with a p row, stocking-st 3 rows.
Inc row: K2, (m1, k2) to end.
P 1 row.
Rep last inc row once (20 sts).
Beg with a p row, stocking-st 15 rows.
Dec row: (K2, k2tog) to end (15 sts).
P 1 row.
Cast off.

Ears (make 2)
Beg at lower edge using the thumb method and A, cast on 10 sts.
P 1 row.
Inc row: K2, (m1, k2) to end (14 sts).
Beg with a p row, stocking-st 3 rows.
Dec row: K2, (k2tog, k2) to end (11 sts).
Beg with a p row, stocking-st 3 rows.
Dec row: (K2tog) twice, k3, (k2tog) twice (7 sts).
Dec row: P1, (p2tog, p1) twice (5 sts).
Thread yarn through rem sts, pull tight and secure.

Antlers (make 2)
Note: antlers are worked in garter-st.
Beg at lower edge using C, cast on 8 sts.
Inc row: Inc, k to last st, inc.
Rep last row once (12 sts).
Cast off 4 sts at beg of next 2 rows (4 sts).
Garter-st 2 rows.
Cast on 3 sts at beg of next 2 rows, knitting the 4th st of these rows tbl (10 sts).

c row: Inc, k to last st, inc.
ep last row 5 times more (22 sts).
ast off 8 sts at beg of next 2 rows (6 sts).
arter-st 2 rows.
ast on 3 sts at beg of next 2 rows, knitting
e 4th st of these rows tbl (12 sts).
arter-st 2 rows.
ast off 4 sts at beg of next 2 rows (4 sts).
arter-st 2 rows.
ast on 3 sts at beg of next 2 rows, knitting
e 4th st of these rows tbl (10 sts).
arter-st 2 rows.
ast off 2 sts at beg of next 2 rows (6 sts).
arter-st 4 rows.
ec row: K2tog, k2, k2tog tbl (4 sts).
1 row.
nread yarn through sts, pull tight and
ecure.

ail
sing the thumb method and A, cast on 8 sts.
eg with a p row, stocking-st 15 rows.
ast off.

Making up

ody
ace two halves of body together matching
l edges. Join row-ends and stuff, leaving
eck and lower edge open.

ase
n base to lower edge of body and sew
ase to body all the way round, adding
ore stuffing to base if needed.

Head
Join row-ends of head and stuff. Bring
marker at cast-on edge and seam together
and over-sew cast-on sts. Place cast-on sts
of head at centre front of neck with seam
underneath and join, adding more stuffing
to neck if needed. Sew back of head to neck
by taking a small horizontal st from head
then a small horizontal st from neck and
doing this alternately all the way round.

Snout
Join row-ends of snout. Bringing row-ends and
marker together, join cast-on sts. Stuff snout
and with seam at centre underneath, pin and
sew snout to centre of lower half of head.

Hind legs
Join row-ends of hooves and with seam at
centre underneath, join cast-on sts. Join
row-ends of ankle and stuff hoof and ankle.
Join row-ends of leg and stuff. To shape hoof,
take a length of A and sew a large st around
centre of hoof, starting and finishing at centre
back of garter-sts of hoof. Pull tight and knot
yarn sewing ends into hoof. Place body on a
flat surface and pin legs to body. Sew cast-off
sts of legs to body all the way round.

Forelegs
Make up as for hind legs with seam at
centre of inside edge. Shape hooves as for
hind legs. Sew forelegs to body at each side,
sewing cast-off sts to neck.

Ears
Join row-ends of ears and with seam at
centre of inside edge join lower edge. Fold
cast-on sts of ears in half and over-sew. Sew
ears to head pointing in opposite directions.

Antlers
Take a pipe cleaner and fold over ⅜in (1cm)
at top. Place pipe cleaner down centre of
antler with folded end at top. Fold antler in
half around pipe cleaner matching all edges
and starting from the top, join outside edges.
When nearly complete, cut pipe cleaner to
size and fold over about ⅜in (1cm) at other
end. Sew antlers to head in front of ears.

Tail
Make a small tassel in A (see page 122)
and anchor it to inside edge of one end
of tail. Gather round this end and pull
tight and secure. Join row-ends of tail
on right side using mattress-stitch.
Sew tail to back of moose.

Embroidering the features
To make eyes, tie a knot in two lengths
of black yarn winding the yarn round 6
times to make each knot (see page 122).
Check that the knots are the same size.
Tie eyes to head on second row above snout
with 7 clear knitted sts between and run
ends into head. Embroider nostrils in black
taking a vertical chain-stitch for each nostril
at sides of snout with 6 clear knitted sts
between. To begin and fasten off invisibly
for embroidery, tie a knot in end of yarn
and take a big st through work, coming up
to start embroidery. Allow knot to disappear
through knitting and be caught in stuffing.
To fasten off, take a few sts back and forth
through work, inserting the needle where
yarn comes out.

Although all penguins are native to the southern hemisphere, they're not only found in cold climates. The Galápagos penguin lives near the equator. Penguins cannot fly, but they can swim up to 25mph (40kph) catching squid, octopus, fish and krill to eat.

PENGUIN

What you'll need

Measurement
Penguin measures 9½in (24cm) in height

Materials
Any DK yarn:
50g black (A)
50g white (B)
20g yellow (C)
20g orange (D)
20g grey (E)
Note: amounts are generous but approximate
A pair of 3.25mm (US3:UK10) needles
Acrylic toy stuffing
Plastic-headed marker pins
Tweezers for stuffing small parts (optional)

Tension
26 sts x 34 rows measure 4in (10cm) square over stocking-st using 3.25mm needles before stuffing

Abbreviations
See page 124

penguin

DID YOU KNOW? The male emperor penguin holds the egg on the top of his feet with his belly flapping over it. He does this for nine weeks before the chick hatches.

How to make Penguin

Back of body and head

Beg at base using the thumb method and A, cast on 5 sts.

P 1 row.

Inc row: (Inc) to end (10 sts).

Beg with a p row, stocking-st 3 rows.

Inc row: (Inc) to end (20 sts).

Beg with a p row, stocking-st 3 rows.

Inc row: (K1, inc) to end (30 sts).

Beg with a p row, stocking-st 3 rows.

Inc row: (K2, inc) to end (40 sts).

P 1 row.

Place markers at beg and end of last row.

Shape tail

Inc row: K17, (inc) twice, k2, (inc) twice, k17 (44 sts).

Next and next 2 foll alt rows: P.

Inc row: K19, (inc) twice, k2, (inc) twice, k19 (48 sts).

Inc row: K21, (inc) twice, k2, (inc) twice, k21 (52 sts).

Inc row: K23, (inc) twice, k2, (inc) twice, k23 (56 sts).

Beg with a p row, stocking-st 13 rows.

Dec row: K25, k2tog, k2, k2tog, k25 (54 sts).

Next and next 8 foll alt rows: P.

Dec row: K24, k2tog, k2, k2tog, k24 (52 sts).

Dec row: K23, k2tog, k2, k2tog, k23 (50 sts).

Dec row: K22, k2tog, k2, k2tog, k22 (48 sts).

Dec row: K21, k2tog, k2, k2tog, k21 (46 sts).

Dec row: K20, k2tog, k2, k2tog, k20 (44 sts).

Dec row: K19, k2tog, k2, k2tog, k19 (42 sts).

Dec row: K18, k2tog, k2, k2tog, k18 (40 sts).

Beg with a p row, stocking-st 9 rows.

Dec row: K6, k2tog, k24, k2tog, k6 (38 sts).

Next and next foll alt row: P.

Dec row: K6, k2tog, k22, k2tog, k6 (36 sts).

Dec row: K6, k2tog, k20, k2tog, k6 (34 sts).

P 1 row.

Place markers at each end of last row.

Dec row: K6, k2tog, k18, k2tog, k6 (32 sts).

P 1 row.

Shape next row: Inc, k5, k2tog, k16, k2tog, k5, inc.

Next and next 2 foll alt rows: P.

Shape next row: Inc, k6, k2tog, k14, k2tog, k6, inc.

Shape next row: (Inc) twice, k6, k2tog, k12, k2tog, k6, (inc) twice (34 sts).

Shape next row: (Inc) twice, k8, k2tog, k10, k2tog, k8, (inc) twice (36 sts).

P 1 row.

Cast on 6 sts at beg of next 2 rows, working the 7th st of these 2 rows, tbl (48 sts).

Stocking-st 2 rows.

Shape next row: Inc, k16, k2tog, k10, k2tog, k16, inc.

Next and next foll alt row: P.

Shape next row: Inc, k17, k2tog, k8, k2tog, k17, inc.

Shape next row: Inc, k18, k2tog, k6, k2tog, k18, inc.

Beg with a p row, stocking-st 11 rows.

Shape top of head

Dec row: (K4, k2tog) to end (40 sts).

Next and next 3 foll alt rows: P.

Dec row: (K3, k2tog) to end (32 sts).

Dec row: (K2, k2tog) to end (24 sts).

Dec row: (K1, k2tog) to end (16 sts).

Dec row: (K2tog) to end (8 sts).

Thread yarn through rem sts, pull tight and secure.

Front of body

Beg at base using the thumb method and A, cast on 4 sts.

P 1 row.

Inc row: (Inc) to end (8 sts).

Beg with a p row, stocking-st 3 rows.

Inc row: (Inc) to end (16 sts).

Beg with a p row, stocking-st 3 rows.

Inc row: (K1, inc) to end (24 sts).

Beg with a p row, stocking-st 3 rows.

Inc row: (K2, inc) to end (32 sts).

Change to B.

Beg with a p row, stocking-st 45 rows.

Dec row: K1, k2tog, k to last 3 sts, k2tog tbl, k1.

Next row: P.

Rep last 2 rows once (28 sts).

Change to C.

Dec row: K1, k2tog, k to last 3 sts, k2tog tbl, k1.
Next row: P.
Rep last 2 rows 3 more times (20 sts).
Dec row: (K2tog) twice, k to last 4 sts, k2tog, k2tog tbl (16 sts).
P 1 row.
Dec row: (K2tog) twice, k to last 4 sts, k2tog, k2tog tbl (12 sts).
Cast off p-wise.

Feet (make 4)
Note: feet are worked in garter-st.
Using the thumb method and E, cast on 9 sts.
Row 1: K.
Row 2: K4 turn.
Row 3: S1k, k to end.
Row 4: Cast off 3 sts at beg of next row (6 sts).
Row 5: K.
Row 6: Cast on 3 sts at beg of next row and k the 4th st of this row tbl (9 sts).
Rep rows 1–6 once.
Next row: K.
Next row: K4, turn.
Next row: S1k, k to end.
Cast off loosely in garter-st.

Flippers (make 2)
First piece
Beg at top edge using the thumb method and A, cast on 8 sts.
Beg with a p row, stocking-st 3 rows.
Inc row: K4, m1, k4 (9 sts).
Beg with a p row, stocking-st 3 rows.
Inc row: K3, m1, k3, m1, k3 (11 sts).
Beg with a p row, stocking-st 3 rows.
Inc row: K3, m1, k5, m1, k3 (13 sts).
Beg with a p row, stocking-st 15 rows.
Dec row: K5, k3tog, k5 (11 sts).
Beg with a p row, stocking-st 3 rows.
Dec row: K4, k3tog, k4 (9 sts).
Beg with a p row, stocking-st 3 rows.
Dec row: K3, k3tog, k3 (7 sts).

Beg with a p row, stocking-st 3 rows.
Dec row: K2, k3tog, k2 (5 sts).
P 1 row.
Dec row: K1, k3tog, k1 (3 sts).
Thread yarn through rem sts, pull tight and secure.

Second piece
Beg at top edge using the thumb method and B, cast on 6 sts.
Beg with a p row, stocking-st 3 rows.
Inc row: K3, m1, k3 (7 sts).
Beg with a p row, stocking-st 3 rows.
Inc row: K2, m1, k3, m1, k2 (9 sts).
Beg with a p row, stocking-st 3 rows.
Inc row: K2, m1, k5, m1, k2 (11 sts).
Beg with a p row, stocking-st 13 rows.
Dec row: K4, k3tog, k4 (9 sts).
Beg with a p row, stocking-st 3 rows.
Dec row: K3, k3tog, k3 (7 sts).
Beg with a p row, stocking-st 3 rows.
Dec row: K2, k3tog, k2 (5 sts).
Beg with a p row, stocking-st 3 rows.
Dec row: K1, k3tog, k1 (3 sts).
Thread yarn through rem sts, pull tight and secure.

Beak
Using the thumb method and D, cast on 9 sts.
Beg with a p row, stocking-st 3 rows.
Dec row: K2tog, k to last 2 sts, k2tog tbl.
Next row: P.
Rep last 2 rows twice (3 sts).
Thread yarn through rem sts, pull tight and secure.

Making up
Body and head
Join row-ends of head on wrong side from sts on a thread to cast-off sts under chin, sewing back and forth 1 st in from edge. With work inside out, pin front to back, matching first set of markers where black changes to white on front and second set of markers where white changes to yellow on chest. Leaving base open, sew in place sewing back and forth 1 st in from edge. Stuff head then body, pushing a large ball of stuffing into tail. Join row-ends of base.

Feet
Take 2 pieces of feet and place together matching all edges. Over-sew both pieces together, sewing cast-on and cast-off sts together and sew round toes. Push a small amount of stuffing inside and over-sew straight row-ends. Repeat for second foot. Sew feet to lower edge of penguin.

Flippers
With wrong sides of knitting together, place a first and a second piece of flipper together matching all edges. Slip-st around all edges and repeat for other flipper. Sew flippers to penguin at each side.

Beak
Join row-ends of beak and stuff, pushing stuffing in with tweezers or tip of scissors. Sew cast-on sts of beak to head all the way round.

Embroidering the features
Using grey, embroider 2 rings in chain-stitch for eyes. To begin and fasten off invisibly for the embroidery, tie a knot in end of yarn and take a large st through work, coming up to start the embroidery. Allow knot to disappear through knitting and be caught in stuffing. To fasten off, take a few sts back and forth through work, inserting needle where yarn comes out.

penguin

111

How do crocodiles keep so slim?

How can monkeys live with themselves?

How do giraffes keep so quiet?

Where do penguins go for swimming lesssons?

Techniques

Getting started

Buying yarn

All the patterns in this book are worked in double knitting (or light worsted in the US). There are many yarns on the market, from natural fibres to acrylic blends. Acrylic yarn is a good choice as it washes without shrinking, but always follow the care instructions on the ball band. Be cautious about using a brushed or mohair type yarn if the toy is intended for a baby or very young child as the fibres can be swallowed.

Tension

Tension is not critical when knitting toys if the right yarn and needles are used. All the toys in this book are knitted on 3.25mm (US3:UK10) knitting needles. This should turn out at approximately 26 stitches and 34 rows over 4in (10cm) square. It is advisable, if using more than one colour in the design, to use the same type of yarn as described on the ball band as some yarns are bulkier and will turn out slightly bigger.

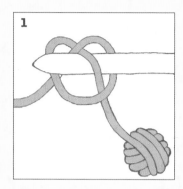

Slip knot

1 Leave a long length of yarn – as a rough guide, allow ⅜in (1cm) for each stitch to be casted on plus an extra length for sewing up. Wind the yarn from the ball round your left index finger from front to back and then to back again. Slide loop from finger and put loop, from back to front on to the needle, which is in your right hand.

2 Pull the tail of yarn down to tighten the knot slightly and pull the yarn from the ball to form a loose knot.

Casting on

Thumb method

1 Make a slip knot. Hold the needle in your right hand with your index finger on the slip knot loop to keep it in place.

2 Hold the needle in your right hand and wrap the loose tail end round the left thumb, from front to back. Push the needle point through the thumb loop from front to back. Wind the ball end of yarn round the needle from left to right.

3 Pull the loop through the thumb loop, then remove your thumb. Gently pull the new loop tight using the tail yarn.

4 Repeat until the desired number of stitches are on the needle.

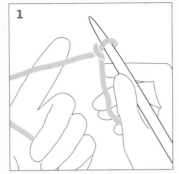

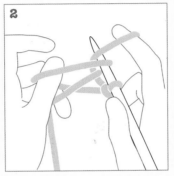

techniques

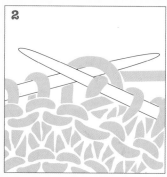

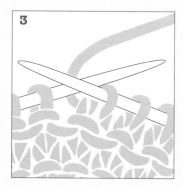

Knit stitch

1 Hold the needle with the cast-on stitches in your left hand. Place the tip of the empty right-hand needle into the first stitch. Wrap the yarn around as for casting on.

2 Pull the yarn through to create a new loop.

3 Slip the new stitch on to the right-hand needle. Continue in the same way for each stitch on the left-hand needle. To start a new row, turn your work to swap the needles and repeat instructions.

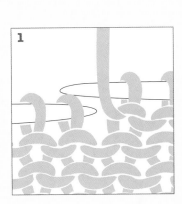

Purl stitch

1 Hold the yarn at the front of the work as shown.

2 Place the right-hand needle into the first stitch from front to back. Wrap the yarn anti-clockwise around the right-hand needle as shown.

3 Bring the needle back through the stitch and pull through.

You might imagine that zebras and pandas don't meet. On the contrary, as well as at the AGM, we meet weekly for tea and sympathy.

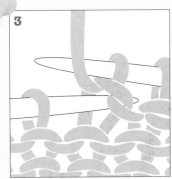

Types of stitches

Garter stitch (A)
Knit every row.

Stocking stitch (B)
Knit on the right side and purl on the wrong side.

Moss stitch (C)

1 Moss stitch (with an odd number of stitches on the needle). With the yarn at the back of the work, knit the first stitch in the normal way.

2 Purl the next stitch, but before you do so, bring the yarn through the 2 needles to the front of your work.

3 With the yarn now at the front, purl the stitch.

4 Next you need to knit a stitch, so take the yarn back between the needles and knit a stitch. Continue to k1, (p1, k1) to the end of the row. This row is repeated.

The patterns in this book only use an odd number of stitches.

Increasing

To increase the number of stitches, there are two methods used in this book: inc and m1.

Inc – Knit twice into the next stitch. To do this on a knit row, simply knit into the next stitch but do not slip it off. Take the point of the right-hand needle around and knit again into the back of the stitch before removing the loop from the left-hand needle.

To do this on a purl row, purl first into the back of the stitch but do not slip it off. Purl again into the front of the stitch before removing the loop from the left-hand needle. You have now made two stitches out of one.

M1 – Make a stitch by picking up the horizontal loop between the needles and placing it on to the left-hand needle. Now knit into the back of it to twist it, or purl into the back of it on a purl row.

Decreasing

To decrease a stitch, simply knit two stitches together to make one out of the two stitches or if the instructions say k3tog, then knit three stitches together to make one out of the three stitches. To get a neat appearance to your finished work, this is done as follows:

At the beginning of a knit row and throughout the row, k2tog by knitting two stitches together through the front of the loops.

At the end of a knit row, if these are the very last two stitches in the row, then knit together through back of loops.

At the beginning of a purl row, if these are the very first stitches in the row, then purl together through back of loops. Purl two together along the rest of the row through the front of the loops.

Intarsia

This technique is used when knitting blocks of colour. Use a separate ball for each block, remembering to twist the old and new yarns at the back when changing colours to avoid holes (**diagram below**). Then weave in the ends at the back with a tapestry needle when finished.

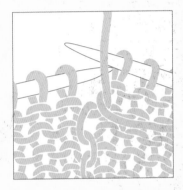

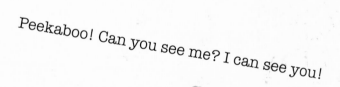
Peekaboo! Can you see me? I can see you!

techniques

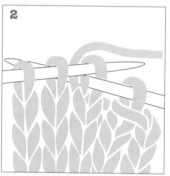

Casting off

1 Knit two stitches on to the right-hand needle, then slip the first stitch over the second and let it drop off the needle. One stitch is remaining.

2 Knit another stitch so you have two stitches on the right-hand needle again.

3 Repeat process until only one stitch is left on the left-hand needle. Break yarn and thread it through remaining stitch.

Koala is inconsolable. We've cast off. It's over.

Sewing up

The animals in this book are put together using simple sewing techniques.

Mattress stitch
Place the pieces to be joined on a flat surface. Lay them side by side, with right sides towards you. Thread a needle with matching yarn and sew the pieces together with small, straight stitches, back and forth. The stitches form a ladder between the two pieces of fabric, creating a flat, secure seam **(diagram right)**.

Over-sewing
Pieces can also be joined by over-sewing on the wrong side and turning the piece right side out. For smaller pieces or pieces that cannot be turned (such as the elephant's tusks or the animals' bases), over-sew on the right side.

Join row ends
Join row ends on all the animals by sewing back and forth one stitch in from the edge.

Wiser beasts know it has only just begun.

techniques

Making tassels

1 Take a piece of stiff card, approx. 3in (8cm) wide, and wrap yarn round it several times. Secure this bundle with a separate length of yarn threaded through at one end, leaving long ends, then cut the bundle at the opposite edge.

2 Keeping the bundle folded in half, wind a separate length of yarn a few times round the whole bundle, including the long ends of the tie, approx. ¾in (2cm) below the fold, to form the head of the tassel. Tie the two ends of this length of yarn together tightly. Trim all the ends of yarn at the base of the tassel to give a tidy finish. If you want a more bushy tassel, unroll and separate the strands of yarn.

Embroidery

To begin embroidery invisibly, tie a knot in the end of the yarn. Take a large stitch through the work, coming up to begin embroidery. Allow the knot to disappear through the knitting and be caught in the stuffing. To fasten off invisibly, sew a few stitches back and forth through the work, inserting the needle where the yarn comes out.

Long stitches
Embroider nostrils, crocodile's teeth and some mouths by sewing long stitches.

Chain-stitch
Embroider crocodile's mouth and panda and penguin's eyes in chain-stitch. Bring the needle up and reinsert where it last emerged. Pull the yarn through to form a small loop and bring the point of the needle out at the end of the loop. Keep the yarn under the needle point and then pull the yarn through. Continue in this way to make a chain of stitches.

Back-stitch
Embroider monkey and hippo's mouth in back-stitch. Bring the needle out at the beginning of the stitch line, take a straight stitch and bring the needle out slightly further along the stitch line. Insert the needle at the end of the first stitch and bring it out still further along the stitch line. Continue in the same way to create a line of joined stitches.

Eyes
1 Make a loose single slip knot and then wind the yarn around five more times, making a total of six times. (The diagram below shows the yarn being wound three more times.) Pull the knot tight.

2 You now have an oval-shaped eye. Make 2 and check that the knots are the same size. Tie eyes to head in position as stated in the instructions. Run ends into head.

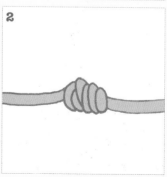

Stuffing and care

Spend a little time stuffing your toy evenly. Acrylic toy stuffing is ideal and plenty should be used, but not so much that it stretches the knitting and the stuffing can be seen through the stitches. Fill out any base keeping it flat; for small parts, tweezers are useful.

Washable filling is recommended for all the stuffed toys so that you can hand-wash them in a non-biological detergent. Do not spin or tumble dry, but gently squeeze the excess water out, arrange the animal into its original shape and leave to dry.

techniques

Abbreviations

alt	alternate
beg	beginning
cm	centimetres
cont	continue
dec	decrease
foll	following
garter-st	garter-stitch: knit every row
g	grams
inc	increase
k	knit
k2tog	knit two stitches together: if these are the very last in the row, then work together through back of loops
k3tog	knit three stitches together
k-wise	knit ways
LH	left hand
m1	make one stitch: pick up horizontal loop between the needles and work into the back of it
mm	millimetres
patt	pattern
p	purl
p2tog	purl two stitches together: if these stitches are the very first in the row, then work together through back of loops
p3tog	purl three stitches together
p-wise	purl ways
rem	remaining
rep	repeat
RH	right hand
RS	right side
s1k	slip one stitch knit ways
s1p	slip one stitch purl ways
st(s)	stitch(es)
stocking-st	stocking-stitch: knit on the right side, purl on the wrong side
tbl	through back of loop(s)
tog	together
WS	wrong side
yb	yarn back
( )	repeat instructions between brackets as many times as instructed

Conversions

Knitting needles

UK:	US:
10	3

Metric = 3.25mm

Yarn weight

UK:	US:
Double knitting	light worsted

Terms

UK:	US:
Cast off	Bind off
Tension	Gauge

Suppliers

Sirdar Wash 'n' Wear Double Crepe
Sirdar Bonus DK
Robin Double Knit

About the author

Sarah Keen was born and brought up in Wales in the UK. She discovered a love of knitting at a very early age: her mother taught her to knit when she was just four years old and by the age of nine she was making jackets and jumpers.

Sarah now works as a freelance pattern designer and finds calculating rows and stitches challenging but fascinating. She is experienced in designing knitted toys for children, having made several for her nephews and nieces. She also enjoys writing patterns for charity and publishes them at home. Sarah is passionate about knitting, finding it relaxing and therapeutic – and very addictive! This is her first book.

Your heyday is not over yet, Hippo.

Index

index

To place an order, or to request a catalogue, contact:
GMC Publications Ltd
Castle Place, 166 High Street, Lewes, East Sussex, BN7 1XU
United Kingdom
Tel: 01273 488005   Fax: 01273 402866
Website: www.gmcbooks.com
Orders by credit card are accepted